The Yogurt Man Cometh

Tales of an American Teacher in Turkey

by
Kevin Revolinski

Çitlembik Publications 102

Kevin Revolinski's articles and photography have appeared in the *Chicago Tribune, Sydney Morning Herald,* and *Wisconsin State Journal.* He is the author of *The Wisconsin Beer Guide* and several works of short fiction. He lived in Turkey in 1997 and 1998 and has traveled back there several times since. Now he lives in Madison, Wisconsin, but it can easily be said—to quote *Pulp Fiction*—"He walks the earth."

Fifth printing, April 2013

Library of Congress Cataloging-in-Publication Data

Revolinski, Kevin.
    The yogurt man cometh /Kevin Revolinski.-5th ed.-Istanbul:Çitlembik
Publications, 2013.
224 p.
ISBN: 978-9944-424-01-1
1.Kevin Revolinski–Turkey–Diaries. 2. Turkey–Social life and customs.
3. Turkey–Intellectual life. I.Title.
LC:DR432 2013   DC: 297.209561

Cover art: Suat Veral*
Cover design: Devrim Gülşen
Author photo: Kristin Abraham

Printed at Ayhan Matbaası
Mahmutbey Mah. Deve Kaldırım Cad.
Gelincik Sok. No: 6 Kat: 3 Bağcılar, İstanbul
Tel: (0212) 445 32 38
Certificate number: 22749

In Turkey:
Şehbender Sokak 18/5
Asmalımescit-Tünel 34430 Istanbul
www.citlembik.com.tr
Certificate number: 12369

In the USA:
Nettleberry LLC
44030 123rd St.
Eden, South Dakota 57232
www.nettleberry.com

* Suat Veral makes traditional Turkish Karagöz puppets out of camel skin. His work can be found in Istanbul's Grand Bazaar, or he can be contacted directly (in Turkish) at suatveral66@hotmail.com.

Table of Contents

To my grandparents

Acknowledgements

My deepest gratitude and affection to all who played a part in this story—friends, students, strangers, and yogurt sellers—but especially to Sister Mary Paynter, my Virgil through the inferno of a life change to teaching, Sister Jean Richter for a critical eye, Anne Porter for being the first to suggest I had a story, Erica Chiarkas for encouragement and making the first compilation in her classroom, Dad for the steady stream of email and archiving, Mom for packages that actually made it through customs, Bryan and Tina for giving me nephews and letting me off the hook, Marty and Sarah for enduring the eternal couch crasher, Vince and Michelle for a place to live before and after, Norma for endless airport transfers, the readers of my emails who gave an egoist an audience, Linda and İffet for being family, Chad and Bob for being the best travelmates ever, Nancy, Carol, Rachel and Didem at Çitlembik for making this happen, Grandpa G. for the blueberry and bacon supply, Grandma R. for the inspiration to travel, and finally Grandma G. for the inspiration to tell stories—she would have loved this one.

The Yogurt Man Cometh

It's Turkey. Too tired to go out for absurdity? Not to worry – they deliver.

It's early on a Saturday. I am slow getting out of bed but at the sound of the door buzzer, I leap into my jeans and race Chad down the hall of our apartment. We don't get a lot of unexpected visitors at the door.

There is a man, unshaven but friendly-looking enough. Having had so many experiences with kind and generous Turks, we have become naively conditioned to expect everyone here to be trustworthy. He smiles and breaks into a spiel in Turkish. Whoa, slow down there, my friend. We warn him that we know very little Turkish and he hesitates for a moment, and then starts over in what Turks call *Tarzanca* or Tarzan language, Turkish spoken without conjugating verbs or using proper articles and such. Probably like most everybody we meet, he assumes we are German tourists. "*Almanca?*" they usually ask.

He indicates his bag of goodies. I manage to decipher occasional words from a long stream of Turkish: "milk," I hear, "cheese," "yogurt." Ah, a door-to-door yogurt guy! The *kapıcı*, the building manager, provides similar to-the-door service for the neighbors. We can leave money in a basket outside our door and the *kapıcı* will go and buy fresh bread for us every day. We have even seen packages in our neighbors' baskets from the supermarket downtown. So here is a guy who maybe wants us on some kind of yogurt route.

He sees our confusion and acts. He points inside and we gesture to him to come in. He declines, hesitant as all Turks are about entering someone's home with their shoes on. But he directs me from the door. He keeps saying a word that we don't know. I go to the cupboard. Ah, he's thirsty. I bring him a glass of water and he downs it but is not sated. He says some other things and I am back in the kitchen, pointing to things and checking for his reaction. I open the cupboard and he nods with excitement. I feel like a trained rat. He points and repeats this strange word. I grab a small pot. He says something else. "Bigger," I understand. OK, a pot. But a bigger one. I find one under the sink. "*Evet, evet.*" Yes, yes. I bring it to the door and he points to it with relief as though now we all understand. Bemused, I hand it to him. He opens his bag, unscrews a large bottle of white goop and pours it in. Whoa. Hold on there, fella. He deftly empties another into the pot before I can stop him. We now have a HUGE pot of yogurt. Um.

And he wants money. Um. Well, we surely don't eat a lot of yogurt. Definitely not damn near two gallons of it. We tell him no and he smiles politely showing us the obvious: we already have it. "Now pay up." Um. I call to my other house-mate, "Bob? Get the dictionary." The man is patient, but I can see it draining from him as Bob pages through the dictionary and we try to piece together the words to tell the man that we hadn't understood what was happening. We don't want the yogurt. "But you have the yogurt. I cannot take it back now." Hm. OK, how much? "500,000 lira." Sigh. A cheap lesson, get the money.

Chad and I return with a 500,000 bill. Now he is annoyed. "Not 500,000. 500,000 *per kilo.*" He squints at the pot. "That's six kilos. Three million." Now that is a lot of clams for a bucket of what more than likely will go to waste. Now comes the standoff. No, we will not pay three million for a bucket of yogurt. Arguing and gesticulations. He keeps waving his arms at the pot, which we keep trying to hand back to him. Take the pot. Keep it. Look up "keep," Bob. How did he say "pot" before? Look up "pot." We don't want the yogurt.

"OK. Two and a half million."

It's not the money. We just don't want it. This unintended haggling goes on for some time until his partner comes up the stairs. By this time he is down to one million and a half.

The partner is fuming and for a moment I am nervous. But there is a door between us if necessary. He says he cannot take it back and sell it because it has been in our pot. I'm thinking, hell, it's yogurt. It's bacteria culture, for heaven's sake. And judging by the looks of these guys I doubt if their operation would pass any government health inspections.

"We don't want the yogurt."

"You must take it."

A battle of wills. Now in a rare moment of assertiveness, I am fuming. "*Bak.*" (Look.) "*Yoğurt...u sev..miyorum. Yoğurtu ist...emi...yorum. Yoğurtu yemiyorum.*" (I don't like the yogurt. I don't want the yogurt. I don't eat the yogurt.) "*Anladın mı?*" Do you understand? We are shoving it back and forth through the door and I fear we will spill it. We will not budge now. This yogurt is going back if we have to leave the pot on the stoop and slam the door. They are, however, still on our threshold. Finally, the partner disappears, cursing no doubt. The other one stands there smoking a cigarette with daggers in his eyes. Nope. No yogurt. Take it. Take the damn pot.

Then our hero arrives. The *kapıcı*. Unlike that of some of the Turkish women we have observed up to this point, this woman's authority does not diminish in the presence of a man. She tells the guy off. "One and a half million? That is ridiculous. And that is NOT six kilos." She lets him have it and he doesn't meet her eye. A rather emasculating moment for him no doubt. He fumes and puffs a bit but she stands firm now between us. He leaves with the pot and we see out the window that he is using a spatula to transfer the yogurt to the jars in the back of a truck. Our *kapıcı* scowled until he disappeared down the steps with the pot, and the woman across the hall is now leaning out anxiously. Once he is gone they both look at each other and laugh. We are sighing with relief and thanking her. She shrugs it off and warns us in gestures and *Tarzanca* to just close the door next time. We, of course, feel stupid for having let him go so far as dumping his fare into one of our own containers.

The man returns with the empty container and brushes past the *kapıcı* on his way out. Chad bellows a cheery "*İyi günler*": Good day! Back inside we slap each other on the back for not being taken. The guy had known we had no idea what was going on. "Boy, they sure were ticked off," says Bob.

I think about that for a moment and how in the States I would be a little nervous that they might come back and be vengeful about it. But I know better here. "Know what the funny thing is? Somewhere a couple of yogurt guys are driving around really ticked off at the Germans."

Arrival in Ankara

The captain announced—first in Turkish and then in English—that we would be landing in ten minutes, yet I could see no sign of the city I had been told was home to over three million Turks. The gently rolling hills below revealed the fabric of agriculture, but I could discern no farms or farm machinery. The uncultivated areas were a dusty brown, speckled with tiny, sparse clumps of green. Could there be a city down there or had I been deceived when I accepted the job?

"It's a desert, right? Don't they ride camels there? Are you sure you want to live with Arabs?" From the moment I accepted a teaching position in Ankara, I learned how little the average American knew about Turkey. To be fair, I knew little other than its location on a map and that it was once part of the Ottoman Empire. Knowing that I knew nothing at least put me on the path to find out. What puzzled me most as I sold off many of my belongings and then stood with my life in two suitcases, was that I was not afraid of what I might find there.

A private school had hired me to teach conversational English to Turkish middle- and high-school students. An apartment and two roommates would be provided for me, along with furniture and basic household items. I would have health insurance and a free lunch every day at school. I wasn't sure what to ask about. What's Turkey like? How could they explain a culture in a job interview? How would I answer a question such as "What is America like?"

13

I grew up in a small town called Marshfield, Wisconsin. With fewer than 20,000 people, it could hardly be called cosmopolitan. But something in me had always wanted to go far beyond the grassy meadows and dairy farms and see the rich variety of cultures in the world. Maybe I could blame this wanderlust on the tattered collection of decades' worth of *National Geographic* in our basement as I grew up, or uncles who traveled for their jobs. Whatever the cause, the world called to me, but I had never answered, never. I settled into an office job and counted the days between my annual two weeks of vacation.

I hated that job. One Saturday morning I attended a live broadcast of National Public Radio's *Whatya Know?* Host Michael Feldman takes a few moments to talk to audience members: what do you do? I felt a sinking feeling. How would I answer that question? What did my job have to do with anything I loved or was at least interested in? I was suddenly embarrassed and sat praying he would not choose me. I made a resolution to do something about that and went back to school to get a teaching license. A year and a half later I was faced with the job search and came across the University of Northern Iowa Overseas Recruiting Fair for Educators. Overseas? Why not? Rather than working all year to enjoy a few weeks of travel later, I could actually LIVE in some exotic place where just walking to work or the grocery store would be traveling.

I set off for Cedar Falls, Iowa, on a cold bleary weekend in February. I went knowing that with no teaching experience job offers might be few. I hoped for something in Latin America; I had always wanted to go beyond my high school Spanish. When I arrived at the fair, I found three interview invitations in my mailbox: Honduras. Excellent. Venezuela. Outstanding. And... Turkey. Turkey? I shrugged—all interviews were good opportunities. But my lack of experience indeed was significant and, in the end, the only offer I received was from Turkey. As a Turk might say with a resigned shrug, "Ah, *kısmet!*" My fate, my destiny.

Six months later, I met my roommates-to-be at O'Hare in Chicago. My travelmates were the two young men who looked as if they had just taken deep breaths and were holding them. Chad Blair hailed from Chicago, Bob Wilson, from Milwaukee, and I had said goodbye to my parents two hours earlier at an airport in Madison. Although I had left home years before, something about my greeting tomorrow eight hours before my family would, made a much bigger impact on them. It was like college all over again as I met roommates who were chosen for me.

We sat in separate seats aboard a half-full Turkish Airlines flight. When we were airborne, the man next to me leaned over and asked me something in Turkish. My look of panic raised his eyebrows and he smiled. "I'm sorry. I thought you were Turkish." He introduced himself as John. He wrote it for me on an airline magazine; it was a Turkish name meaning "life" or "soul" and was spelled C-A-N. "The C is like a J in English." Can gave me my first Turkish lessons as I passed a nearly sleepless ten-hour flight to Istanbul. He was a private pilot for a company in America and was returning to visit his family in Istanbul. With my arrival growing closer, the questions came pouring forth: What's the food like? What things do you see on TV? Are there movies? Where are the best places to visit? What will be different? He admired my enthusiasm and I admired his warmth.

Linda Fenton, one of the two women who had interviewed me in Iowa and the American assistant department head at our new school, Büyük Kolej, had asked us to look after her two boys, who had been visiting their grandparents in Kansas and were traveling on the same flight. Eren and Koray both spoke fluent Turkish; I was now the child. Kicking back with a Game Boy, they were well-behaved, experienced travelers.

There was time to chat and room to move about, so I did. Chad offered me some trail mix as I stood near his seat for a while asking questions. For both of us, this was our first professional teaching job. He had just graduated from the University of Illinois. When he stood up to go to the restroom I could see he was slightly taller than I, six foot, dark hair cut in a utilitarian way, brown eyes and a slight build.

Bob was sitting a few rows away, and where Chad exuded a sort of casual tranquility, Bob was more animated. At 27, he was a couple of years younger than I, shorter and stocky, with dark hair short enough to be spiky and a lazy eye that often corrected itself. Bob already had some teaching experience and would be working at the elementary level. Though we were all already excited about our coming adventure, Bob's enthusiasm and openness were infectious.

I squirmed, sleepless, in my seat long after the lights went out. With daylight slipping toward us from the horizon, Can woke up and we continued talking. We exchanged addresses and I promised to call him if I ever came to Istanbul. He recommended I do so as soon as possible.

Upon arrival we by-passed customs and went directly to our connecting flight to Ankara. After ten hours, the hour-long flight felt only as long as a takeoff and a landing. The approach to Ankara revealed nothing. The airport seemed like the center of an empty field in Wyoming. We stepped from the plane to the tarmac and on into the main terminal, which seemed small for a capital city.

Just inside I found Linda hugging her boys. She kissed each of us on both cheeks and introduced us to her boyfriend Hasan. He was built short but solid like a wrestler, spoke no English, but smiled and gripped my hand in a way that reinforced my wrestler suspicions. Though Linda was nearing 40, her blond hair, blue eyes, and a lightness about her suggested she was 15 years younger and gave her an air of mischievousness.

"Those waiting for arrivals are supposed to wait outside. But. Well...." She grinned and shrugged it off as unimportant. When we took our baggage through customs to be searched, we could see a mass of people just outside the front doors, craning their necks to see inside.

A school van was waiting for us and Linda went to wave for it while we stood at the curb with our luggage as Hasan shooed away all the would-be porters. The other new teachers—Joan, a fifty-something blond elementary teacher from Minnesota, and Jim, a mildly sardonic high school teacher from Canada who had come along as a last-minute hire and romantic interest of Joan's—had joined us.

The sun was painfully bright and my lack of sleep had brought on a throbbing headache. The heat was intense, but the air was dry. I studied the crowd as we loaded the baggage. The men wore moustaches, plain pants, buttoned shirts, and leather shoes. Some women wore Western dress, while others wore long robes and covered their heads—but not their faces—with the traditional veil of Islam. The head coverings were loose and many revealed the wearers' hair, so they didn't seem so unusual to me, but rather reminded me of my great-grandmother, who frequently wore her babushka when outside. People laughed in reunion with loved ones, while others sobbed at departures or shouted last words to travelers disappearing through the front doors. The concrete walls and overhang collected a swirling echo of Turkish that left me dazed. Taxis honked, someone whistled shrilly, and I was shaken from my trance.

We left for the long ride into the city but just outside the airport we were waved to the roadside by a couple of police officers toting submachine guns. For Americans, the first sight of law enforcement carrying large automatic weapons in hand is unsettling. We waited apprehensively for several minutes as the driver showed some papers and talked with the officers. After a lengthy pause and no explanation, we were sent on our way again.

Signs of civilization began to emerge, first simple houses and then larger concrete apartment buildings. It finally became clear that we had penetrated the "outskirts" when the buildings became high-rise apartments and occasional domed mosques with one or two minarets, the towering needles that are to mosques what steeples are to churches. The landscape rose and fell dramatically; in some places the world dropped away to a small valley full of houses roofed with red tiles. Lawns and trees were scarce, but there was an abundance of roses and bougainvillea in front yards — it could have been Mexico or Wyoming; but as we drove deeper into the city, Ankara began to look more like a modern metropolis. Hordes of taxis and buses converged on us as we entered a commercial district of tall office buildings and a square that featured a brightly lit advertising screen much like those in Times Square.

Jim spoke up to the entire van: "Are they open about homosexuality here? I just saw two guys holding hands." Linda explained that it is common for men to walk arm over shoulder, and that there was nothing sexual about it in Turkish society. Pedestrian traffic was abundant and a couple of blocks later I saw two old men walking down the street arm in arm like old friends.

Everywhere I looked, the Turkish flag—a bright red banner with a simple white crescent moon and star—was prominently displayed. Some massive flags hung down three or four stories on the sides of buildings and one banner featured the stern face of an older man with a receding hairline and large bushy eyebrows that curled up at the ends. This was Mustafa Kemal Atatürk, the founder of the modern republic. "Whatever you do," Linda said, "never say anything bad about him. He is highly revered." I thought of Big Brother peering down upon the people.

Jet lag left my head bobbing as we wove in and out of streets ever closer to our apartment. We turned into a steep road and the engine whined as the driver downshifted to make the grade. İzci Sokak: Scout Street, my pocket dictionary revealed. Our street had no curb or gutter and seemed like a hastily laid strip of asphalt that connected Fethiye, the lower residential street, to the busier Filistin Sokak up from our apartment. The neighborhood itself rose sharply with the terrain; apartments were planted one just slightly higher than the next, the way farmers terrace crops on hillsides. We stopped before a three-story brick building. The front gate was painted white, and a metal fence, intertwined with bushes from within, thrust up from a stone wall. The postage-stamp yard must have been watered because it was greener than the rest of the city I'd seen thus far. Interlaced through the fence and an arching lattice over the gate was an explosion of rose blossoms. Home? I thought to myself.

Linda left us after the bags were unloaded, and we began exploring our second-floor apartment. My new home extended from the front of the building to the back. Walls were white, and floors were concrete with a superficial hardwood covering in the living room and tiles in the other rooms. The large living room in front featured a balcony, as did the kitchen behind that. We poked around like children sizing up an old house for play.

Outside the kitchen were cherry trees and clotheslines along the balcony railing. Past the kitchen was a study, and beyond that a hallway with three bedrooms, one large and two small. One of the two bathrooms was more of a closet with a porcelain bowl built flush with the floor with a tread on either side for a person's feet. The three of us looked at each other with half grins.

"Um... I guess that's a toilet."

To our relief, the other bathroom had a traditional toilet as well as a washing machine and a bathtub with a shower. The washer emptied into the tub, which in turn drained into a hole in the floor via a hose from the tub drain. We laughed at the irony of being in a new culture and finding ourselves closely scrutinizing the plumbing arrangements.

Bob returned to the living room and I could hear the unmistakable babbling of a television. He shouted down the hall. "Hey, we have cable!"

Nestled into the artificial fireplace was our connection to the ether, and we scanned through to find half the channels in Turkish and the other half in a variety of languages, three in English.

"OK, who gets which room?"

Bedrooms were decided by an elaborate decision-making process—commonly known as rocks, scissors, paper—and Bob emerged victorious, claiming the large bedroom at the end of the hall for himself. I beat Chad in a best-out-of-three and claimed the first room, closest to the study. We started unpacking. Each of us had brought some books, Bob had some specifically for teaching, and I grimaced at my own oversight. We laughed as each of us withdrew a Lonely Planet guide to Turkey. We were all excited about using them as soon as possible. Finally, Bob pulled out the music.

"You brought a CD player?"

"With speakers. So we have music." Already it was "we" and I appreciated Bob's immediate generosity. Chad was no different; his laptop and printer were ours if we ever needed them.

My head was growing heavier by the minute and so I piled my things in the corner of my room, laid down a sheet on the bed, and fell asleep, even though Linda had recommended that the best way to beat the jet lag was to stay awake until a normal sleeping time. Three in the afternoon? Close enough.

The Citadel

Linda picked us up later that afternoon in the same school van with another teacher who was starting her second year at the school. Jane was a few years older than Linda, with curly red hair and a slight Texas drawl. She lived just at the bottom of our hill in another school apartment.

Our primary destination was the Citadel in Ulus, the old part of the city. Unlike Ulus, the Republic of Turkey is historically rather young. The Turks had been there, of course, for some time, invading the Anatolian plain (what is now central Turkey) from Asia in the late eleventh century and then in 1453 finally conquering what was then Constantinople (now Istanbul, as the song says). This was the final blow to the preceding empire of the Byzantines. At its height, the Ottoman Empire, named for the Turkish tribe that founded it, stretched into Europe and the Middle East. In the early twentieth century, the then-waning empire sided with Germany and eventually fell to the Allies in the Great War, and what is now Turkey faced being carved up by the victors and handed in part to Greece. The Greeks marched almost as far inland as Ankara. But General Mustafa Kemal earned the name Atatürk, father of the Turks, when he reunited his people, drove the Greeks from the mainland, and effectively laid the borders of a new nation. He became its first president, and changed Turkish society, government, and even the language itself in progressive ways. Linda was understating it when she said he was revered.

Before Atatürk passed over the obvious Istanbul and made Ankara the capital city with the founding of the republic in 1923, there was not much more to the city than a citadel high up on a hill and about 30,000 people. In only seventy-five years it had grown to over three million. Shops and artisans line the narrow roads up to the Citadel. Just outside the gate, a covered market overflows with nuts and spices. Dried figs and apricots, pistachios and almonds, red pepper and henna powder are displayed in baskets and boxes, and the merchants stand by their scales measuring out purchases with aluminum scoops. They are quick to give samples, and we picked up handfuls of pistachios before entering the Citadel.

The Citadel—in part dating back to Roman times—now only protects a collection of old stone and wooden houses and a few shops and restaurants. Stones recycled from earlier structures still display words chiseled in Latin. The old ramparts offer an excellent view of the modern city around them. Back outside we started down a narrow road that buzzed with work: men carried heavy loads on their backs, bundles of clothing; hawkers, unintelligible to me, shouted their wares to passersby; a boy with a tea service deftly balanced in one hand scurried through the crowd like a mouse; coppersmiths tinkered and tapped out kitchenware and decorative platters. We passed a photographer's studio with several portraits in the front window. One showed a young boy in a uniform with a white feather in his hat and a mild smile on his face.

"Linda, they have marching bands here?"

She looked where I pointed. "No, that's the Muslim circumcision ceremony."

"Oh."

Linda stopped to talk to a shopkeeper who wore a long robe that looked more Arab than Turkish; the front of it showed where he wiped the work from his hands. He sold repolished metalware and we crowded into a tiny room lit only by a bare bulb hanging from its wires. Shelves lined the walls, floor to ceiling, and everywhere there was the dull glint of metalware: water decanters, tea services, pots, pans, engraved platters. He spoke to a woman with a headscarf who immediately squeezed past us to the street. We sat on short, square wooden stools with wicker seats and she returned moments later with a young boy carrying a tea service. The tea—*çay* (starts with "ch," rhymes with "eye")—came in tiny, clear glasses. Each rested on a metal saucer with two sugar cubes and a teaspoon. My first thought was, "How much will the tea cost?" But tea is sacred in Turkey—business doesn't occur until it has been served and rarely is there a price tag attached. The glass burned my fingers as I raised it to my lips to blow across it a bit before sipping.

The man went about the room holding up objects for our appraisal. Linda had been here several times before and recommended it. Every time one of us looked interested in an item, he immediately set to polishing it. Some of the more tarnished items, he assured us, would look brand-new once he worked on them. He convinced Chad, who selected a large platter with intricate Arabesque designs etched into it. Chad suggested it would look good over the fake fireplace back at the apartment. The old man promised it would be ready the next day.

Food was the next adventure. I grew up in a beef and potato family, with a freezer full of venison restocked every hunting season. Though beef is not hard to find in Turkey, chicken and lamb predominate. And with 99% of the population being Muslim, pork products are available only in import shops or large supermarkets, and presumably only in areas frequented by foreigners. The *şiş kebap* is a primary menu item and a term and cooking style not unfamiliar to most Westerners.

A common form of lamb is *döner*. The vertical spit which

I had associated with the Greek gyros, I was told, with no small amount of indignation, was a Turkish invention. Fat drippings smoking in the cooking fire ruin the taste of the meat, so an Ottoman chef had the idea of skewering the meat on his sword and holding it next to the fire rather than over it. Whatever its origins, the device dominates the streets, and in every restaurant we passed, I could see the towering cones of rotating lamb's meat (and sometimes stacked chicken breasts) in the front windows. I never acquired a taste for lamb and, in fact, by the end of the year even the smell of it made me shudder. But that first day in Ankara, Linda introduced me to an exception.

At the edge of Ulus was a restaurant that served the best *İskender kebap* in Ankara. İskender, named for its creator Alexander of Bursa, is made with long thin strips of lamb laid over fresh *pide* bread and then smothered with tomato sauce, yogurt and browned butter. Warm butter dribbled down our faces as we dug into our first truly Turkish meal. Black-tie waiters served with very formal efficiency, as though we were royalty. Coca-Cola was brought out to us in glass bottles— something I hadn't had since aluminum and plastic took over in the States—and the waiters filled our glasses as if it were an elegant wine. This wasn't a tourist production; I saw that all customers received the same service. But we *were* tourists, and Bob, whose camera hadn't left his hands since we had left the apartment, leaned over his plate and took a picture. I was right with him and held my plate up next to my face for the next shot.

Classroom Rules

Just before sunrise I was rousted from my dreams by a long, musical cry from outside. I marveled at how loud the man's voice could be and realized that it was through amplification. It was the call to prayer, the first of the five daily reminders of Islam.

Our first new teacher meeting was after lunch and we walked to school, down one hill and up another just over three blocks away. We were stopped at the gate by security, who called someone, then passed us along. Linda met us and led us to a classroom to begin.

"Really, all you have to do is keep them talking in English. That's your job." The classroom—concrete walls, marble floor, and no ceiling tiles—echoed like a racquetball court with Linda's instructions. We sat like new students, crammed comically into desks that fit two children side by side. İffet, the Turkish department head, chimed in when necessary. She was a short woman, with short, straight brown hair, kind eyes, and a calm, motherly look to her. She watched us with a warm smile. I remembered how comforting that smile had been in the Iowa job interview. That, combined with Linda's disarming frankness and her knack for knowing when not to take herself too seriously, made the strict formality of the classroom rules less intimidating. A little...

"You will hear the call to prayer during your lessons. Some previous teachers have made light of that. Please. Use your head. One guy last year used to say things like: 'Hey, isn't that number six on the charts this week?' I think you guys know better. It can be pretty loud when the windows are open. But don't close the windows. If someone asks to close them, that's fine. Just ignore it and go on teaching. When you enter the classroom, they should all stand at attention. This will seem weird at first but make sure they do it. They know you are American teachers; if you go soft on them the first week, they'll be hard to keep únder control. You're going to find they like to a talk a bit." (Nervous looks by both us and our instructors as the statement seemed ominously understated to all ears.) "There's a ten-minute break between classes. You don't have to stay in your room during that time. There are lounges on each floor—smoking and nonsmoking.

"Chad and Kevin, there are thirty-two students in each class and you will divide them and take them to separate rooms for conversation. Your plans will be the same. Each class period you will have to make an entry into this book." She held up a thin, oversized blue book. "According to the Ministry of Education, each hour of each day of the school year must be entered. You enter the date, the name of the course, a brief description of the lesson, and then sign your name at the bottom. If it is a two-hour class—and most of yours will be—then you must fill it in for both hours. Since it is technically one class, both of your signatures must be there, so you need to send the book to your partner each hour. You can ask a student to do that. They will be very eager, of course. They love to help their teachers. On Monday mornings you need to be here for the flag ceremony. We will assemble on the playground according to class. Stand with your class and make sure they stay in line. We sing the national anthem and then wait to be dismissed to class. The same thing occurs before dismissal on Friday afternoon. Foreign teachers only need to be here when you have class. If your schedule doesn't start until ten, then you don't need to come in until class starts. Unless it is your duty day, of course. Duty days are..."

The instructions poured forth and I jotted down some notes, but feared I would forget all the procedures by the time class started. "That's about it."

"Just that?" I thought.

"Oh, and one more thing. Don't steal anybody's nose."

"What?"

"It'll make a kid cry."

She was referring to the sweet little game adults play with small children, tweaking a kid's nose and then thrusting the thumb out between the two first fingers. "This—," she held her hand up for show and tell in case we had forgotten, "—is about the most offensive gesture you can make in Turkey."

Jim pointed to the Atatürk picture above the whiteboard in the front of class. "Is *he* in every class?" The portrait, along with the words to the national anthem, were in every classroom. I looked up at the intense blue eyes staring down at us and sat up straight.

If the portrait were not enough to encourage good posture, "the Mooder" was. At the mere mention of him, Linda's mischievous smile seemed to say, "Wait 'til you see this guy." İffet and Linda took Jane and us to his office where a secretary picked up her phone to announce us. His door was wide open and we heard him answering in a booming voice which made the use of a phone seem ridiculous. We knew everyone walked lightly around him. Müdür Bey, literally Mr. Principal, was an imposing man, corpulent but spry, with large features and serious thick-lensed glasses. His thin graying blond hair receded a bit. He rose from his chair with a toothy smile of receding gums and a ruddy face that looked as if he had recently been angry. He strode around his desk and crushed each of our hands. The three of us had practiced a simple Turkish phrase that morning, "*Memnun oldum*," the equivalent of "Pleased to meet you."

Spoken like children, no doubt, it nevertheless raised his eyebrows and broadened his smile. The smile disappeared when he looked at Jane and asked something. Linda translated, "Why don't you ever speak Turkish?" There were uncomfortable smiles and he turned to us again.

"He is very pleased to have you here," said Linda in translation. We expressed our gratitude. He said something more with a great belly laugh and Linda chuckled as he looked on, prodding her to repeat it. "He says that you are all very handsome. He will find you Turkish wives." At this he nodded enthusiastically and slapped our backs, partially to guide us to the door.

Linda explained what we had done so far and what we would be doing the rest of the day. He followed as far as the hallway where Zeynep, an attractive blond teacher, was passing, and stopped her to introduce us. He wasted no time in mentioning that we were handsome and the search was on for our wives. She was single. The insinuation was not lost.

The school building accommodated the sloping hills of the neighborhood; four floors of classrooms rose up, and four floors rested down the hill, as if the building had been horizontally cut in two and slid apart. The front gate entered on the first of the upper four floors, while the rear entrance was down the hill on the true first floor with a terraced plaza. The playground occupied the roof of the lower four floors and functioned as tennis or basketball courts, and assembly area.

In the lobby, the janitors in their sky blue jumpsuits greeted us as Linda provided a tour. They moved in small groups like Willy Wonka's Oompa Loompas, rushing about changing light bulbs or mopping. Downstairs were the cafeteria, snack bar, indoor swimming pool, gymnasium, small library and a room with a ping-pong table.

"This is where the table tennis team practices."

"A *team?*" I asked. "You mean *ping-pong* is a sport here?"

"Ask Müdür Bey. He loves to play. I hear he's pretty good actually."

Our final stop was the office of Rumi Bey, the man who, with his two sisters, owned the school. We waited a while in his reception area before finally being invited into a room full of beautiful woodwork. Rumi Bey had an expensive suit, the taut tanned skin of someone accustomed to luxury, and white hair. He was soft-spoken and professionally kind. A custodian brought in our drink orders. It was one of the few times I ever met him and we made painstaking small talk before leaving for home. An hour later, back at the apartment, the phone rang. I answered as my Turkish book had instructed me, praying that an English speaker was on the other end. "*Efendim?*" Literally translated it means "my sir." It is also used as "What?" when asking someone to repeat something you didn't hear. To my relief it was Linda. "I'll pick you up at 7."

The road passed along the upper ridge of the city to a tower that rose up like a giant flashlight above a small two-story shopping mall called Atakule.

"The restaurant is across the street but there's a great view of the city here." We were joined in the elevator by a young couple and their five-year-old daughter who kept singing, "*Güzel Ankara, güzel Ankara!*"

"What's she saying?"

"Beautiful Ankara."

And so it was. The city lights sloped down before us and shimmered toward the horizon. Far away was a glowing white mosque at the center. We tried in vain to find Ulus, really the only landmark we were familiar with at the time.

Across the street at the restaurant, we were immediately attended by black-tie waiters. Looking around at the elegant decor I wondered how much it would cost.

"The great thing about this place is that you can see what you are going to eat before you order."

Looks deceived; this was a cafeteria. We pointed our way through various meat and vegetable dishes beneath a glass counter near the kitchen. But we couldn't remain restaurant-helpless the whole year, and we each began our own language efforts, rolling the new sounds awkwardly in our mouths to the waiter's delight, never to his amusement.

Chad, it turned out, was vegetarian. If it weren't for the chicken on the menu the predominance of lamb would have forced me to become a convert myself. The meal was excellent: lentil soup, chicken stew covered with cheese, cold vegetable salads, spinach and eggplant among other things. But one thing we all found peculiar was the waiters' eagerness to clear our plates. We had to remain alert lest they thought we were finished and whisked away our half-eaten meals.

Pistachios and One-Way Streets

Our first official task was to copy yearly plans. These large spreadsheets are sent to the Ministry of Education where someone probably puts them in a big file cabinet where they sit with the lesson plans from the past fifty years. Bureaucracy comes directly from the top, not locally. In education in the United States, the states themselves resist federal involvement and even at the local level there is resistance to the state requirements. During my teacher training I had practiced writing lesson plans, planning units, even whole quarters, but here I was writing up the entire school year.

As Bob was an elementary teacher, Chad and I reported to a separate classroom to start going over the papers. We spent a lot of time simply writing in chapter titles from a textbook. Our hands cramped up as we struggled to write a large amount of information into tiny calendar squares. Special holidays, such as Youth Day, had to be highlighted and plans were written in to show how we would teach the kids about Atatürk in every class that day. Though the whole process was time-consuming, it didn't require a lot of mental effort; with the exception of my tenth-grade class, it was only a matter of filling in squares more or less with the previous year's information.

"This shouldn't take too long," I commented.

"What if we finish early? Maybe we could get away for the weekend."

31

"Yeah, before classes start. Let's ask Linda before we leave today."

Sitting in the English Department office, we were able to meet everyone who stopped by. Several Turkish teachers taught English, and in the course of the day we met them and chatted about what to expect from the school year and Turkey itself. Two were named Ebru and to distinguish them, Chad, Bob and I amongst ourselves referred to them as Ebru Blond and Ebru Dark. Dilek, also a fellow teacher and good friend of İffet, warned us with a smile. "Be hard with the students the first week. If you're not, they'll know they can take advantage of you."

Gaziosmanpaşa, our neighborhood, was situated on one of the highest points in Ankara. From the third floor of the school, the entire city lay before us. Most buildings were three stories high and created a mosaic of red-tiled roofs that spread in all directions, rising and sloping sharply with the landscape. The tin roofs of the mosques shone in the sun between sharp minarets that thrust up to the sky, and the call to prayer which rang out from blaring loudspeakers rose up to us. I could see the distant Citadel atop its rocky hill, and far beyond that a chain of low-lying mountains seemingly bare of vegetation. Chad and I stood for a while, silently admiring it all. Later in the afternoon after Linda and İffet approved our plans (thus freeing us up to travel for a long weekend), we took to the streets to explore.

Traffic was noisy and consisted mostly of taxis and buses. As we crossed a street, a taxi turning up a hill spun out on the smooth asphalt surface right in front of me as it fought to make the grade. "Can you imagine what happens if they have ice in the winter?"

I was carrying a pocket dictionary and we were trying to read signs. Chad stopped me, "What's that say?"

"Steel doors. Hm."

Chad looked beyond it and pointed. "There too? They must use a lot of doors around here."

It was true; the block we were standing on had what appeared to be *three* steel door shops. The further we explored the neighborhood, the more that appeared to be a pattern. Like businesses seemed to congregate. Two fruit markets faced each other; where there was a barber, another could be found two doors farther down. I wondered how they survived. But I appreciated the presence of a neighborhood. The butcher, the tailor, the druggist, were all within a few blocks of my home. Only parks were lacking. The buildings were crowded together like subway commuters in rush hour leaving few spaces, and in what few remained there were foundations going in.

A couple of old men walked by arm in arm. "Even the people are close together!" I said.

Bob asked me if I knew where we were. "Not a clue. We just crossed... Tek Yön Street... Say, didn't we cross that a while back? Are we going in circles?"

Bob looked at the sign. "I think maybe it means one-way. See the arrow?"

"Yeah, but look at the traffic." Cars were parked on both sides of the street and a taxi had just turned down the lane opposite another oncoming car.

"Well..." Bob was doubtful.

Chad said, "Look it up."

"Tek yön: one-way."

"Bob wins."

"Yeah, but... look at the cars!"

"Maybe you should loan them your dictionary."

We wandered in and out of streets until hunger set in, and then turned toward school and our apartment beyond that. Chad was the guide; I was already completely turned around. "Look for the Sheraton." He pointed, and the circular hotel towered above the rest of the buildings marking the edge of what I considered our territory. Just across from the school on the back side was a convenience store with an English name—Lights Market. We stopped to buy sodas. The owner asked us a question in Turkish. We stood mute like children asked to confess to having looted the cookie jar. "Um..."

He thought a moment. "Eh... what... country."

Bob told him and then added in Turkish. "Teachers..." drawing it out long enough to point at each of us. "... Büyük Kolej."

He shook our hands. "Erdal."

"*Memnun oldum,*" we each stammered and added our names. He grinned at our Turkish. We thanked him and took our leave, promising in gestures to return the empties. He waved the matter away.

Though we had been told that Turkish wasn't necessary in our jobs, we had committed to learning as much as we could. Armed only with a couple of phrase books and an optimistic *Turkish in Three Months* guide, we embarked on a tongue-twisting journey. I started with the basics "please," "good day," "thank you," and "I want," and used the local shops as testing grounds. But it wasn't easy. İffet had told me that, in fact, it used to be written in Arabic script. Another of the legendary Atatürk's accomplishments was that in the late '20s he abruptly told the Turkish people they should no longer use Arabic script. In three months he effectively erased it from the entire country and replaced it with Latin script with a few extra modified characters to accommodate some special sounds. But despite the clarity of the script, it offered many challenges.

The difference that I found most challenging was thinking backwards. In English we generally start with a subject, then the action and all the rest follows. "I went to..." In Turkish, verbs come at the end of the sentences. My challenge was to figure the verb in my head, then hold onto it until I composed the rest of the sentence. Until I learned to reverse my thinking, I was often left forgetting what it was I had wanted to say when I first opened my mouth. It is almost comical in literal translation: "Tuesday on friends my with store the to go did I." If I wanted to speak Turkish, I needed a system.

We put charts on the wall in the study and thus created "The Grammar Wall." Using index cards as labels, the house became a Turkish kindergarten. The door – "*kapı*," the window – "*pencere*," and a book – "*kitap*." And sheet by sheet the grammar wall spiraled outward through verb tenses and vocabulary.

That night we dined a couple doors down from the school at a restaurant we had noticed on the day's walking tour. "You know, we need to start buying groceries."

Chad was right. We couldn't eat out the entire year. We ate a sort of elliptical pizza made with cheese and egg on top or meat similar to pepperoni. It was cheap and filling and we knew how to ask for it.

On our way home we stopped where a local market spilled out onto the sidewalk. All along the front were the overflowing crates of fresh produce which the clerk would weigh in scales dangling from the awning. It was like point and click without the computer as one of the grocers, a mustachioed fellow with glasses and a few extra pounds under his apron, followed our fingers through the fruits and vegetables. Inside we wandered through the three aisles learning vocabulary off food labels.

"Check this out: sour cherry juice. Apricot." We picked up one of each. By observation I learned to gather eggs into a plastic bag and close it with a knot.

No one other than the produce man outside had seemed

to notice us as out of the ordinary and so, emboldened, I stepped up to the deli man and asked for a half kilo of black olives. With a great flourish he withdrew a plastic bag and stooped to the barrels. There were three varieties, three prices, and I saw no difference among them. I opted for the mid-range with a point of a finger. With a scoop he filled the bag and flipped it up onto an electronic scale: 1.5 kilos. He smiled broadly as one does when landing exactly on the dollar pumping gas without slowing down, then spun the bag shut and deftly tied a knot in it. He said the price but I was stumped. So he wrote it on a slip of butcher paper.

The man at the front counter—a big blond man with a moustache, who could have been Karl from Czech Republic—added it all up on paper without a word. The grocer leaned in the front door and told him the produce total. We paid and said Thank you and Good night.

"He gave me one and a half kilos. I asked for half," I lamented.

"You mean, you *think* you asked for half."

Bob was right. The words for "one-half" and "and a half" were completely different. The grocer had heard the "and a half" and assumed I had mumbled the "one." A delicious lesson, it turned out, as I ate a third of them with a loaf of fresh bread back at the apartment, washing it all down with my immediate addiction, the ironically sweet sour cherry juice.

On the rug in the living room we had the guidebooks and a map laid out.

"We have enough time that we can get somewhere relatively far away," Bob said.

"I asked Linda and she said that if we take a bus overnight, we can arrive at the Mediterranean in the morning," said Chad.

Bob seemed uncomfortable, so I asked him, "Something wrong?"

"Are either of you guys having stomach problems? I'm just wondering if maybe I've got something starting."

Chad and I responded in unison, "Ask Linda!" We laughed. As much as it sounded like a silly radio call-in show, we immediately recognized and appreciated how much we relied on Linda.

Chad bent over the travel guide. "What's in Fethiye?" We shuffled through a few pages and read passages out loud to each other and were soon in agreement. We would be week-ending on the Mediterranean.

The next day, in preparation for our trip, I called the Ask Linda line for a place to buy allergy medication. Linda recommended a pharmacy near school. An old woman smiled up at me from a chair by the door, and seated along the front window were two men, about thirty and sixty, and a young girl of eleven or twelve. I explained to the pharmacist in Tarzan Turkish that I was a new teacher at Büyük Kolej. Her face lit up and she became friendlier. We matched my medication with a box from the shelf behind the register and I paid her. I ended up paying $10 over the counter for what in the States would have cost $100 and required a prescription. I thanked her and walked out, pleased at a successful Turkish transaction.

Two steps from the door I heard tapping at the window. I turned, hesitant, thinking perhaps I had taken the wrong thing or paid the wrong amount. The old man in the window was tapping the glass and waving. My attention was drawn to his hand which was missing all four fingers to the second knuckle. I could see the old woman through the door also waving and I said "goodbye" to them all, thinking that I had slighted them all by only saying it to the pharmacist. But they persisted and I waved again, bemused. The gesture they were giving me was with the palm of the hand faced down, bending up and down at the wrist—and for all intents and purpos-

es in MY world—shooing me away. But every time I turned
to go, the waving became more insistent. I stood like a child
unsure which way the bathroom was and wanting to be
excused. Somewhere in the dim back room of my head, I
remembered something about gestures from my travel guide.
On paper, much like stereo instructions, gestures often don't
come out clearly. But I had a Eureka moment: the gesture
meant "come here" and in the street is the equivalent of a
hitchhiker's thumb.

I returned to the store and they offered me pistachios from
a large platter on the coffee table. I took three. Now by anybody's standards, that was pretty funny. Who the hell takes
three nuts, barely enough to fill a tooth? The old man
laughed, grabbed my wrist with his stubby fingers, and filled
my palm. In patient Turkish, like talking to a child, the pharmacist explained that her daughter, the little girl, would start
fifth grade at my school the next week when classes started. I
pointed to myself and since I couldn't say "I will teach sixth
grade" I simply said "six." I think they understood I wasn't
commenting on my age or IQ. I asked her name and she said
something I couldn't repeat, but I nodded "ah." We stood
nodding—I uncomfortably, they with warmth—and said
nothing. Finally, I turned to the little girl with a stern look
and said in English in an almost scolding tone, "I guess I'll be
seeing YOU in school." Then I smiled and they all laughed,
though the little girl did so hesitantly. I chuckled all the way
back to the apartment, munching on my pistachios.

Fethiye and the Hidden City

That night we were off on our first travel adventure as we hopped an overnight bus to Fethiye on the southern coast. For $12 I expected marginal service akin to Greyhound in the States so I was surprised when we were served drinks and given a coupon for a free meal at one of the nice waysides. When we woke up in a different city, the attendant came around with a bottle of lemon-scented cologne which was to be splashed liberally on the face, neck, and arms. Without it the bus crowd surely wouldn't have smelled so fresh.

Sleeping on the bus meant missing most of the horror of the road. "Two-lane highway" was merely a suggestion—three cars abreast can still fit on hills and blind curves and the bus driver never hesitated to pass when I was looking. Outside the station, we were immediately accosted by pension owners and *taksi* drivers like a swarm of flies buzzing in the Turkish-English hybrid we immediately took to calling Turklish. One man pursued us to the last, even walked us into town pointing things out though we had never invited him: Güler Bey (Mr. Güler), a sixty-ish pension owner wearing whites and dress shoes and carrying a rolled newspaper in one hand. He had white hair, a moustache and sharp eyes and was able to spot potential tenants for the night and then have them inspecting a room at the pension before they knew what hit them—like us.

It was late in the tourist season, there were three of us, and as we had already walked all the way from the bus stop carrying our bags, it must have been clear we were capable of looking around. His offer was one million lira per night—six bucks for each of us, breakfast included. We found a small but clean room with three beds, a balcony, and a bathroom with hot water. Breakfast—the traditional Turkish breakfast of hard-boiled eggs, tomatoes, cheese, olives, honey, and lots of fresh bread—would be served in a rooftop restaurant half-shaded by an overhanging trellis of vines. Any attempts to play the seasoned traveler were surely seen through by our host; we were like kids, speaking in a new code and exploring an exotic playground.

Only an hour after arriving, we were on board a boat that resembled a small ferry. We had begun a walking tour, starting with the curving bay of the marina, when a lanky, barefoot boy had leapt from a gangplank as we were passing and had us running back to the pension for our swimming trunks. The boy was the eldest son of the family that commanded the boat. The deal was all day, food provided, for one million lira for what he called the Twelve Island Tour. I never counted the islands but in the course of the six-hour trip we stopped at four coves to swim. We soaked up sun on the upper deck while below our feet, the bow curled the incredible deep turquoise into a foamy white. Mountains covered with pines ran right down to the water, and pebbled beaches appeared intermittently along the shoreline. At one stop, our captain pointed out a partially-submerged stone building that dated back to Cleopatra's time; now it was simply the backdrop for a swim.

Lunch, a buffet of local fish and vegetables, was served on board. With our hunger sharpened by swimming and sunshine, we devoured our food ravenously. Back in the rooftop garden, we sprawled in comfortable chairs to watch the sunset over the bay of Fethiye as we read, wrote in our journals, and slowly became drunk on a sour cherry liqueur we had bought on the walk back.

In the morning, Güler Bey sat teaching us a few key break-fast words as we ate. We set out to explore the area around Fethiye by hopping a *dolmuş*. The *dolmuş* is a large van with a few seats that can sometimes hold as many as twenty-five peo-ple uncomfortably; its name literally means "stuffed." It can resemble a circus clown act when the entire van has to let out the guy in the back corner. In rural areas, travelers may find themselves sharing the ride with a goat or a dog but this day it was a couple crates of tomatoes. The driver waited patient-ly as an old man loaded them. The passengers never appeared to lose patience despite the heat and clearly uncomfortable crowding. The *dolmuş* follows a set route like a bus but is only slightly more expensive and stops on command. Often it is the best connection between a series of villages for the intermit-tent commuters who are not frequent or numerous enough to merit a full-sized bus.

Our destination was the gorge at nearby Saklıkent, which means "hidden city." Over centuries, ice-cold water carved through the mountains to make a shadowy and narrow canyon of polished stone, striped with the colored layers of its sedimentary composition. We rented rubber shoes and hiked through a magical planet of sandy passes and outcroppings that stood like abstract marble sculptures bathing in waters milky white with minerals. At some points, we slid several feet down natural chutes like water slides; in others, the stone closed in around us to reduce the sky to a thin curving path of azure above. We took a few chances when the going got tough and climbed some rather slippery and potentially dan-gerous waterfalls. We were not alone in the gorge, of course, and found ourselves conversing with people from various parts of the world and lending a hand when we converged on difficult passes. Our exploration ended abruptly when we came to a sheer twenty-foot stone face. With shrugs we start-ed back the way we came as the angling rays of the sun penetrating into the chasm turned the sandstone layers to gold.

When we re-emerged from the gorge, we ate *pide* pizzas on platforms that hung over the main branch of the river, a tumbling rapids that was too powerful and deep to hike up, but which widened and mellowed when it met with the stream we had just explored. Restaurants kept their soda bottles cool in crates wedged among the rocks under our feet.

As we passed through a market beyond the canyon, a young woman at a fruit stand offered me a sample of her produce. She held out a round green item with a skin the texture of a tree leaf. She smiled at my bemusement and showed me how to open it. A fresh fig. I felt foolish when I realized that I had never seen a fig that hadn't become a Newton already. On the return ride to Fethiye, a young man turned when we began conversing in English.

"Where are you from?"

Bob answered for all of us and we added our standard enthusiastic responses to "What do you think of Turkey?"

Erkan was a student from Istanbul. We complimented him on his English and by the time we stepped off, our new friend had insisted on being our guide to a beach the next day.

From our rooftop that night we saw a spotlight blazed on a columned tomb entrance and stone stairs halfway up the mountain overlooking the town. As we admired the view, the call to prayer—that lingering and haunting voice of the muezzin rising up from the town and echoing back down off the stony hillside—caused me to catch my breath.

It turned out that none of us was about to ignore the call to the tomb and we were soon hiking through the winding streets, looking in screenless windows at Turkish families eating late meals or watching television. Old women in veils eyed us suspiciously from darkened porches. At occasional turns and through breaks in the periphery of rooftops, we could see our destination growing larger. When we reached the bottom of the tomb steps, we found a streetlight and a pay booth. No one was there, but the gate was open. We decided to pass, hoping that if we were doing something wrong, our bumbling Turkish would absolve us. "Hello. I am a teacher. I like football. Bread! Bread!"

Before we took our first step three men stepped into our pool of light. "*Merhaba. Nasılsınız?*" they asked. "Hello. We are fine. And you?" we replied. They were very friendly and invited us to go up, where we took pictures of each other but found nothing more than what we could see from the street. We were nervous for no good reason other than being in a dark street in a strange land with no language skills, and they seemed amused by that. One spoke some English and introduced himself as Veysel, a university student from the "east west" of Turkey near Mt. Ararat. He meant the western part of Eastern Turkey. He was Kurdish.

This was a word we had been quickly conditioned to react to by some of the Turks back in Ankara in casual conversations during our orientation. "You don't want to travel in the East." The Kurds, an ethnic minority, are spread throughout eastern Turkey and into neighboring countries like Iraq and Syria. When the revolution of 1923 founded a new republic, it included everyone within the new borders. In Atatürk's vision Kurds were citizens of Turkey, "Turks." But this was a far cry from the separate nation they were promised by the Allies after the fall of the Turkish Ottoman Empire after World War I. Many Kurds have assimilated and some estimates claim that 40% of the Turkish population has at least some Kurdish blood. A previous prime minister, Turgut Özal, even openly proclaimed his Kurdish ethnicity. But some Kurds support separatism. And some, such as the PKK, the Kurdish Workers' Party, were willing to fight for it. Like in so many ethnic conflicts in the world, this one escalated. The Turkish military sought to crush the PKK; the PKK used hidden bombs and ambushes for its own ambitions. The Kurdish language and television and radio transmissions were prohibited. The southeast became embroiled in a war, one that caused many deaths for both sides and mostly for those caught in between, and the whole matter fed a growing distrust of Kurds and the East. And we had been given that distrust. Now we had to decide what to do with it.

The truth was, at the time the PKK *was* dangerous and responsible for several random bombings in population centers. But being Kurdish is not the same as being a member of the PKK. We were looking into the face of a young man who was working a summer job far from his home and befriending strangers. His body was tensed with excitement as he walked with us, and he spoke with an intensity that showed his impatience with his lack of English—English that was enviable when I considered our inability to get much beyond short greetings in Turkish. When he found out we were teachers, his eyes lit up even more. He was studying to be a teacher and insisted we write to him and visit his city, Diyarbakır, some day. We already knew what the reaction would be from our co-workers who, to be fair, were only worried about our safety. At that time, Abdullah Öcalan, the leader of the PKK, was still at large, accused of being responsible for varying totals of deaths in the thousands, depending on who you asked. (Since his capture in 1999, the situation has improved and prohibitions on Kurdish language and culture have been overturned.)

Veysel and his friends walked with us to the harbor, where we bought them beers and sat on a curb by the dark water. He hid the beer when we took photos, explaining sheepishly, "My father would kill me." Alcohol is forbidden by Islam. He was fascinated that we would be away from our families for an entire year. Just being in Fethiye for a couple of months was difficult for him. I thought about how I had effectively moved out when I went off to college. Several of the single women teachers at my new school, well into their twenties, still lived with their parents.

We parted with handshakes and addresses and headed back to our pension. But we didn't get far before we heard loud Turkish music and followed our ears to a block-long section of street that was closed off by plastic patio chairs and people dancing. We watched from the far reaches of the streetlight, enjoying the music that seemed so strange to us. It was a man and a synthesizer, as is common in Turkey, playing a canned Latin-sounding beat with the melody of a reedy instrument. A group of children came out of the party with a long piece of telephone wire and were attempting to jump rope. They were bickering among themselves, so we teachers took charge. In minutes, we had them in pairs taking turns while Bob and Chad turned the rope. So adorable and swarming on us, shaking our hands, telling us their names, so excited to play with the goofy strangers who spoke no Turkish save perhaps the numbers to count each successful passing of wire beneath their feet. The girls all had palms dyed with henna for the celebration.

We noticed a couple of young boys about seven years old, wearing white suits and hats that looked like marching band uniforms. I remembered the portraits back in Ankara: a circumcision celebration. Judging from their angelic expressions, it was a *pre*-party. When the party began to dissipate, we left the wire behind and the children followed us en masse to our pension, drifting off one by one until there was only one boy left to wave crazily and cry *iyi akşamlar*, good evening, to us.

For our last day in Fethiye we hopped another *dolmuş* to Ölüdeniz, the Dead Sea, a pocket of Mediterranean water nearly landlocked and waveless. We found Erkan waiting with a backpack at the entrance. In some conservative Muslim countries, men and women had separate bathing areas.

Imagine my surprise when I found that not only was the area shared by both genders but it was top-optional. It was an initial shock, but quickly became mundane. As Americans, many of us are conditioned to either snicker or take prudish offense, and I think many would presume Turks to be even worse. Everyone should receive a humbling dose of travel.

Erkan and I snorkeled together for a couple of hours and we spent the rest of the time lounging on a beach of small rounded pebbles. He had even had the foresight and generosity to bring fruit, Doritos, and a box of sour cherry juice for all of us. The small food stands, he told us, were overpriced. We sat under an olive tree eating bread and sipping juice. He had a mildly formal air about him, smiling but not laughing much. He was well-mannered and polite in the way people are who have strict parents, but it wasn't the air of aristocracy. When he began to talk about the history of the area he had the diction of a guide. He swept an arm toward the curling strip of bathers. Alexander the Great had hauled all the stones there to build the beach in honor of Cleopatra. The small, rounded stones, he told us, were brought by ship all the way from Egypt.

Mistaking Erkan's accent, Chad thought he had said "by sheep." Embarrassed, he admitted he hadn't been quite sure how many herds of sheep it would take to haul such a large amount of pebbles from Egypt. Erkan rode with us back to Fethiye and then left us after we promised to look him up in Istanbul.

That night Güler Bey walked us to the bus and we gave testimonials to potential customers as they arrived. We shook hands, took a couple of pictures together with our host and patient language instructor, who donned my canoe hat for the photo, and then we were off on the overnight bus back to Ankara. In the space of one weekend, we had met a couple of pen pals and potential hosts from various parts of Turkey. Crazy world, but friendly.

School Begins

Albert Einstein used an analogy to express his idea of relativity. "Put your hand on a hot stove for a minute, and it seems like an hour. Sit with a pretty girl for an hour, and it seems like a minute. THAT'S relativity." I'm not sure that brings me much closer to understanding Einstein, but I have a similar concept regarding traveling. Condensed time. Back in my old office job, months could pass before I looked up at a calendar and thought, "Where did the time go?" When I travel for a week or two it seems that every minute is alive and vibrant, as if all the excitement from six months of my regular routine occurs in a matter of days. So much can happen in an afternoon on a bus through the unfamiliar that, after a week of it, it feels as if I have lived a month. Suddenly the answer to "How was your weekend?" becomes a long unraveling narrative, like an endless parade of circus clowns climbing out of a *dolmuş*.

All the teachers were returning from their vacations and Müdür Bey needed to speak to everyone. Linda warned us that it was more a love of speaking than a need. We crowded into one of the faculty lounges, pulling in chairs from other rooms until there was no place to move. When "the Mooder" (as the three of us had taken to calling him) entered the room, all rose to their feet and ceased their chatter and took their seats only after he did. I took a good look at the person so many spoke of with a sort of subtle fear. Whether he were Mr. Principal or not, he would have commanded a room. His

47

ruddy face and slightly sagging jowls were in the serious mode and gone was the toothy bellowing laugh. The Sultan began to speak. And speak he did—for over two hours. It was a lecture more than a meeting. Linda was supposed to translate for us and at first she did. Welcoming the teachers back, a few words about the coming year and then Linda sighed and sat back in her seat. "What's he saying?" I asked.

Linda shook her head. "I'll tell you when he says something important."

We sat like squirrelly children in church, passing notes for distraction. Jane, Jim, Joan, Linda, Chad, Bob and I were all misbehaving but the Mooder never missed a beat. He lectured on until even our little distractions became boring.

After the meeting we ate in the cafeteria. The English teachers sat together with the Mooder. I poked at a stuffed eggplant uncertainly. "What's this?" I held up what I thought was milk.

"*Ayran*. Yogurt."

"To drink?"

"They add water and salt it a bit. It's good."

I forced part of mine down and moved on to a cold bean salad and finally the tiny donut balls soaked in syrup. When Jim joined us, he stared at his food a moment, then brought out his keys and began dangling them above the tray.

I wondered; Linda asked. "What are you doing, Jim?"

"I'm seeing if it is safe to eat. You see, depending on the way the keys spin, it might not go with my own energy." I thought he was nuts, and the Mooder leaned to İffet for the translation. He laughed loudly and looked at Jim, unsure of whether he was serious or not. Jim came to the conclusion that the food would not go well with him. I wondered what the keys had to say about his cigarettes. The food went OK with me, and for teachers it was, in fact, a free lunch every day.

We worked in the office in the afternoon and then attended a teacher social on the patio outside. Servers passed among us with platters of finger food and small paper cups full of soda. I examined one platter full of an orange-colored mash rolled into tiny cigar shapes. "Any idea what this—?"

Bob shrugged, already eating it. "Ask Linda."

It was *çiğ köfte*, meatballs made with raw ground meat and hot spices. The spiciness allegedly kills anything in the meat. They were delicious but as the heat rose up in my face, I quickly washed them down with Coke.

Two women in their late 40s, who could only be sisters, approached and Linda introduced them as Rumi Bey's sisters, who held some kind of vague administrative duties. Jim and Joan joined us. Jim was avoiding the food. As if he knew that, the Mooder beckoned our attention from across the patio, waved his keys over his drink, and fell into a bellowing guffaw. Jim smiled.

Many of the faculty were women, and none wore Muslim head scarves. Several held important positions, including Ayşe, the assistant principal and disciplinarian for the middle grades, a tall and heavyset blond woman with a pretty face and the air of authority. The English department was run by women as well. The men were generally distinguished, gray-haired professors in nice suits. I smiled at an attractive young woman standing off to the side and Linda told me she was the new German teacher.

The following night we prepared to attend a wedding with Linda. Someone on the faculty had invited everyone to a small hotel downtown. All dressed up, we waited for Bob, who emerged from the bathroom and closed the door behind him. "Don't worry, I lit a candle."

"Still not feeling well?" In fact, I had started to get a general grumbling downstairs. Linda called it the "crudruk," a vague malaise that often struck new arrivals as their bodies adjusted to the new foods. The light of the candle flickered through the frosted glass window of the bathroom door. "Bob has made fire" became a general house warning.

The hotel was in a nearby commercial neighborhood on Tunalı Street and we entered a salon where people milled about awaiting the grand moment when the bride and groom would sit down and unceremoniously sign a document. It was strictly a legal affair and I wondered what we were missing by attending a wedding in the city. .

The Mooder saw us, came over, kissed us on both cheeks and then slapped us on the backs. I winced at my sunburn. "Handsome!" he cried. "Turkish wife!"

Bob reached over and took a glass of sour cherry juice from a waiter. Instead of "thank you" he told the waiter, "pleased to meet you."

For the flag ceremony on Monday morning, the first day of school, we stood on the playground to await the Mooder. All the children—dressed in blue jackets and gray slacks for the boys and white shirts and blue skirts or shorts for the girls—stood at attention, warily eyeing the teachers who moved among them to enforce discipline. If the meager audience in the faculty had inspired the Mooder to talk, the squirming masses of students and teachers must have thrilled him to death. Heads bobbed and weaved as if the crowd were a small ocean while everyone shifted their weight from one foot to the other. For over an hour we listened to his voice blare out of bullhorn speakers high on the chain-link fences that surrounded the lot. Linda translated very little, explaining that it was a summary of the rules regarding uniforms and a warning that it was a privilege to be at Büyük Kolej: several students who had not appreciated that fact would not be back this year.

The ceremony closed with balloons being released with tiny fireworks and purple smoke bombs attached, many of which simply burned themselves off the balloon strings and plummeted to the crowd. Then the elementary school music teacher sang the national anthem, holding the mike in one hand and directing the children with the other. The song has the heaviness of Russian music; it starts in a minor key and ends on a resolving major chord. But its march-like quality and the way everybody sings along so fervently in uniform dress, spoke of the solidarity of a military state or something from an Orwellian movie. I found myself humming the song later in the day.

When I entered my first class with Chad all the kids ran to their desks and stood straight at attention. There was some whispering and a simple look in that direction elicited a "Sorry, teacher." Chad and I split them and I took my sixteen students to my own room. They were well-behaved, but tended to talk a lot. I kept reminding myself to play the hard guy. But it seemed unnatural for me to scowl or even yell. I knew they would get the better of me, especially the sixth-graders. They were adorable.

One of them came up to my desk.

"Teacher?"

"Yes?"

"I lose my rubber."

"Er... your *what?*"

"I don't find my rubber."

My eyes went back and forth wildly between the little boy with the concerned face and the rest of the class that looked on calmly. "I... um... Your *what?*"

Then someone cried out, "I find it!" Everyone turned to the girl in the last row. I was more curious to find out exactly what it was she found. An eraser. I chuckled to myself nervously. British English. It looked like we were *all* students.

But a few Brit vocabulary words wouldn't be my biggest challenge. Each class would meet for two hours once a week.

I had fifteen classes. That meant that I had roughly 225 students each week. 225 names, *Turkish* names, to memorize.

The students sat in two-seater desks, more or less a bench attached to a writing surface. Boys sat with boys, girls with girls, and in both cases they sat very close together. Best friends had arms over each other's shoulders. I introduced them to their books and a video series that goes through conversation as painful as bad soap opera writing. Every other week, one of the Oompa Loompas wheeled in a TV and VCR.

If Monday was an easy day—one class in the morning, one in the afternoon—Tuesday was my nightmare. Four two-hour classes on one of two weekdays that the school day extended an extra hour. One of these classes was the tenth grade—25 teenagers jammed into those little desks. From the very first moment I failed to gain control. The students chatted like all the rest but did not respond to my authority. A few of the boys, ties loose, shirts untucked, looked up at me defiantly at first and then with disinterest. But my training had been at that age level, and so I felt confident I could connect with them. At the end of that day, Chad invited me downstairs to play some table tennis.

"What do you think?" Chad asked.

"Long day."

"A trade-off for the easy Monday."

"How was your tenth grade?"

"Tough crowd."

"Mine too."

Chad beat me handily a few times and we returned to the apartment for the day.

Wednesday I met 8E, one of five eighth-grade classes. They immediately took their places and stood so silently at attention that it unnerved me; something was amiss. I told them to sit and they did. A girl in the front row put her chin on her hands and stared at me dreamily and I hoped it wasn't in earnest. Then I looked for my board marker. It wasn't with my books where I had left it. It wasn't in the tray along the bottom of the whiteboard. I found it in a desk drawer and when I went to pick it up the whole room flew into a titter. It came unstuck with a gentle pull leaving behind long hairs of rubber cement.

I sighed, gave a grim smile. I would be learning a lot from this class. After two hours with them I could see theirs was the best English, even better than the tenth-graders. They were smart and outspoken, already addressing me boldly and requesting a change in how conversation class should be run. The dreamy-eyed girl's name was Candan and I understood quickly that she was generally bored with school and looking to give me a hard time to make it a little more interesting.

Towards the end of the week, after meeting most of my classes, walking through the halls became a chore of wading through children who simply wanted to say "Hello, teacher. How are you? I am fine tanks" (no "th" sound). "See you, teacher." Then they would go away smiling back at me and running into each other. Like the people in the streets, the children walked arm in arm, boys leaned on each other, and girls were connected at the hip. The ten-minute break between periods—signaled by a distorted, computerized version of Beethoven's "For Elisa" in place of a bell—was clearly too much time between classes. Most students managed to race down two or three flights of stairs for candy or to the playground to shoot basketball, and then race back to class full of sweat, sugar, and adrenaline.

Thursday I had my first *hazırlık* or prep class, children who had either transferred and were just starting to learn English or had failed English completely the year before. I told them to sit and they stood smiling so I made a downward motion with my hands. They thundered into their desks as though playing Simon says.

"Good morning." A collective response of variably pronounced "gooood morningk" from most, while a few others sat with wavering grins, eyeing their comrades.

"How is your English?" Nervous smiles, one student blurts, "Thank you, teacher." Everyone giggles.

"How are you?"

It sounded like church, a methodical, rhythmic response, "Fine tanks, and you?"

"OK, well, shall we start?" Wavering smiles. "Er... do you have your books?" Silence, then a snicker. "Um... do... you... have... books?" Still nothing. "Do you understand me?" Everyone nods. "Do you understand the process of fission in a thermonuclear reactor?" Fewer nods. A few less certain of their physics. First lesson of teaching English as a second language: rare is the student who answers "Do you understand?" honestly.

We worked through the two hours using pictures from the books, and I was relieved (though not much) that some of the students began to resurrect remnants of English they had learned before. In the hall, I saw Linda and İffet. "Oh my God. The hahzzers..."

"*Hazırlık?*"

"Right! They don't speak *anything*!"

She chuckled. "Trust me: you will really be able to see the progress in them, more so than in the other classes."

İffet chuckled. "Don't worry. You'll do fine."

Being one of the *hazırlık* students myself, I asked about something one of the students had said. "What does *hocam* mean?"

"It means 'my teacher' but it has a sort of religious overtone to it. They aren't supposed to call you that, but a lot of them still do."

On Friday, I noticed one of the sixth-grade girls who looked on the verge of tears. I recognized her from one of my classes. I asked her if she was feeling ill (not "sick." Sick, we were warned, sounds similar to the Turkish f-word and tends to elicit giggles). She shook her head and looked up with crinkled brow and big brown eyes. I remembered not to steal her nose. "Are you OK?"

"No, teacher. I hate this school." She said this not angrily, but sadly. I love the honesty of children; get right to the heart of the matter.

"Are you new to the school?"

"Yes, teacher I have been here for only five days and I just hate it." Good English for a sixth-grader.

"But why? It is a good school."

"Yes, I know teacher. It is so hard." She glanced back and forth, eyes brimming with tears. I crouched to where I could talk to her better and rested an arm around her shoulders.

"But your English is good," I offered.

"I lived in the United States for a few years."

"Ah. Well, look: This is normal. Whenever I go to some place new I feel like that too. But in a week or so you won't even remember. It will get better; I promise. And besides, sometimes hard things are good. They make you strong." I growled and shook her gently. The corners of her mouth quivered upward in a smile. "You'll be OK."

"Thank you, teacher." She left for class as the bell rang, waving back at me. Later on that day, she came up to me smiling. "Teacher? When do we have class again?"

"Isn't it Tuesday?"

"Yes, I think so. See you, teacher." She smiled and ran off. I was left standing with a million bucks.

On the walk home I picked up a new word from the neighborhood children. There are very few playgrounds in the city, and nothing of open spaces, so the streets become soccer fields. As I walked up my hill, I heard the children shout "*Araba! Araba!*" and one child gathered the ball as they all cleared to the side to let a car pass. When I approached, it was almost the same interruption. They stood and stared at me curiously. "*Merhaba,*" I said. They echoed in unison. One little girl tugged shyly at an older boy's sleeve, others stood with the formality children adopt when addressing one's elders. Then I addressed them in plural, "*Nasılsınız?*" How are all of you? "*İyiyiz,*" they replied, we are good. But it came out in a rising sing-song "eeeeeYIZ" in the way some kids will draw out goo-OOD in two tones. They stared after me a moment before returning to play.

Those first few days, I awoke each morning unsure of whether the day before had been real or just something my subconscious threw together for my nighttime entertainment. I called it "casual absurdity." Every once in a while I would see something astounding in the street and people would barely react to it, if at all. I felt as if I was in a Monty Python skit. I walk home and a man is gutting a sheep that he has hanging from a telephone pole. The head stares up at me from the sidewalk. Or down Tunalı Street, women who look like mounds of mismatched fabric fragments move from trash pile to trash pile, collecting what looks like discarded chicken fat. The *polis* officer on my street weeding the flower bed across from his post or kicking a soccer ball around with some kids, all the while with an automatic weapon in one hand. The irony, of course, is that there is nothing quite as absurd as the stranger walking around gawking at another's everyday life. It was my mission not to be that stranger, but at times that was no small challenge.

Bob turned 28 that weekend and we hosted a party both for him and in celebration of a successful first week at school. We practiced the invitation in Turkish and carefully announced it in each faculty lounge during the week. We had waited half an hour in the Mooder's office to invite him personally. He was surprised, but accepted with enthusiasm.

Saturday morning, as I was heading out for some fresh bread, I heard someone shouting *"efendim"* through a loudspeaker out front and then a cry like a warning such as "The British are coming! The British are coming!" Bewildered, I leaned out the window and there was a man on a tractor using a bullhorn to wake the neighborhood. But it wasn't an evacuation call; in the trailer behind him were piles of potatoes and onions. I didn't understand a word he was saying through the thing other than the garbled *"efendim."*

The walk to the market was downhill and I tried to do it without being forced into that run to which a steep hill sometimes brings a person. The uphill walk was amazing; I'd turn the corner and the road seemed right in front of my face like a wall. There was no need for a health club when just the walk there would be twenty minutes of intense climbing.

As I rounded the corner, I heard a loud booming voice. An old man, hunched over, wearing a dusty green plaid sports jacket and a felt hat like a fez, was hobbling down the roadside. He bellowed in a voice like Zero Mostel's: "Balon! Baaaaaaaa-loooohn!" Around his neck, like an extension of his flowing white beard, was a collection of balloons, red, yellow and blue. His sales plea echoed off the building fronts and between each cry he moved a couple of agonizing steps. He clutched a can in one hand and a crutch in the other. His right leg was bent like a bow and I realized that through his Coke bottle glasses, he couldn't even see me or the children who stopped to stare at him.

I rounded the corner and passed grocers and their crates of fresh produce stacked in small terraces out front. Shopkeepers sluiced down the walk with water several times a day to keep down dust and cool the air. Throwing water struck me as something Turks love to do. Something in the way a shopkeeper swirls water out of a cup onto the walk, the gentle motion of his wrist makes it seem as though he is sampling wine and finding it fit for the gutter.

I arrived at the market and proudly asked the grocer in Turkish, "Do you have bread?" Turkish does not use a verb like "to have" to express possession. The word *var* and its question marker *mı?* literally ask "does it exist?" "Hi, Coca-Cola exists?" *Var,* it does; *yok,* it does not. For possession you add a possessive suffix to the item in question. So one is not asking if a person has a car, but rather "Does your car exist?"

"*Ekmek yok,*" he said and then sent me next door. The market was dim, lit by a couple of bare bulbs. I went to the display cabinet in the front window, opened the wooden doors, and the light from outside poured in along with the heat and smell of freshly baked bread. It felt like lying in bed in a patch of golden sunshine in the morning. The loaves were still warm to the touch and I took three. "90,000" he told me and wrote it on a slip of paper to be sure, about 60 cents. On the walk home I couldn't resist. I pulled out a loaf and had it half-eaten before I arrived home. I passed the old man and his collar of balloons; he was only another twenty feet farther than where I had left him. He shuffled along the pavement as black flies circled about his heels.

A Birthday Party with the Sultan

In our final preparations for the party, Chad, Bob and I ran out to the market for some wine and plastic cups. Around the corner was a woman patiently unraveling a bale of wool and it looked as if a giant dog had shed clumps of hair around the yard. She spread it along her sidewalk and hung clumps over the fence. She had taken her mattress apart and was airing out the wool stuffing.

Just down the block something falling from above caught my eye. I turned to see a man deftly snatching a lira bill twisting through the air. Three stories up a woman waited with her hand on a thin rope for the man to fill the attached basket with potatoes. She hauled it up, hand over hand, as we passed.

At Lights Market we found Erdal in his customary position, leaning heavily on his counter, smoking a cigarette. He rose to greet us. We bought some soda and asked for wine recommendations. He ignored the bottles on display and disappeared into the back, reappearing with two dusty bottles. He pointed to the labels and nodded convincingly. *Tamam.* OK. I looked up "plastic cups," piecing the two words together, no doubt unconventionally, and told him I needed 20. He hesitated a moment and instructed us to wait, opened the register, removed a one-million note, and squeezed past us to the door.

First, he leaned to the right into the photo shop next door, saying something quickly in Turkish. He turned to the left then and summoned a teenager who may have been just hanging about; we were not sure, perhaps he was only a passerby. The boy disappeared with the bill, running down the street. Erdal resumed his post behind the register and rang us up, and then we stood there smiling at each other. Moments later the boy returned with a stack of plastic cups and some change which he gave to Erdal.

The party was at 8:00 p.m. and the Turkish guests didn't start arriving until after 9:00. Normal, we were told. Jim and Joan were first to arrive and then Jane and her friend Shala, a petite Iranian woman with dazzling black eyes and accented English. Fearing people from school might not show up for the party, I was glad for the distraction of her conversation.

At 8:30 the buzzer rang and I opened the door on a delivery man who began explaining something. I caught the word bakery, *pastane*, but remained clueless. He showed me a receipt and I thought he was the man who refilled our drinking water jugs. He showed me the receipt again and I noticed the last name of Müdür Bey. I pointed down the stairs and he nodded with relief. In a car outside was a birthday cake for Bob, compliments of the Mooder, which became the centerpiece for our spread of food—homemade garlic/yogurt dip, refried Turkish beans, chips, breadsticks, homemade pizzas, and plenty of beer and wine.

Everyone brought some kind of alcoholic beverage: bottles of wine, vodka, Miller beer. Finally, Müdür Bey arrived with a bottle of the finest *rakı* (rock-UH) in Turkey. *Rakı*, the national pride and drunken joy, is anise-flavored and sweet, but at 100 proof, deceptively strong. It is also known as "lion's milk," because when mixed with water, the clear liquid becomes an opaque white (and also because Islam forbids alcohol—but not milk). It is usually served with an ice cube or two and chilled water. *Yavaş! Yavaş!* Slowly, we were warned, slowly. *Or tomorrow you will be not well.*

The Müdür had entered with his entourage—his wife

Güneş, a prominent member of the parent community named Ahmet, and Ahmet's wife Hilal. Even outside his element, the Müdür had command of the situation. Everyone rose to greet him at the door. The way he drew translators to him with a snap of his fingers or a wave of his hand made him the Sultan. We had concerned ourselves with making the proper impression, and now it seemed the Müdür was our new best friend, kissing us all on both cheeks, praising us before the crowd. He was most impressed, as was everybody else, with our grammar wall. He laughed at the label on the door - *kapı*. İffet locked her arm around my elbow and beamed with pride. Apparently previous teachers hadn't been so interested in the language.

Everyone ate, laughed, socialized, kissed cheeks, and got tipsy by night's end. The Müdür at one point was comparing his foot size with Chad and then our Sultan, red-faced with *rakı*, was wearing cheap Keds knock-offs.

At the end of the night we cut the cake, a fruit-filled, layered monstrosity with sparklers in place of candles. The singing of "Happy Birthday" turned into a language stew, as the crowd included a German, a Scandinavian and an Iranian contributing in their native languages to the Turkish-English mix. As we sat on the couches in the living room, the wine and *rakı* mellowing us like a fireplace simmering down to embers, Esen, one of the Turkish English teachers, began to sing Elvis' "It's Now or Never" in a rich alto. We applauded her and everyone began starting songs which we all sang until they either ended or fizzled out where the words were forgotten. Linda and Bob volunteered to do the American national anthem and the Müdür, without irony, stood at attention with his hand over his heart through the entire song.

When Shala departed she left her number, asking us to call her the next time we had a party. By the time everyone filed out (which took a long time with all the cheek kissing), it was

1:30. But we were so invigorated by good company and good feeling that there was no way we were about to sleep. Linda led a taxi caravan to a crowded disco called *60's*. Hasan, Linda's boyfriend, who was all smiles but no English, bought us a couple rounds of *rakı*. How much 100-proof licorice can a person stand in one night? I thought. We were jostled around against sweaty bodies amidst thick cigarette smoke and loud music. The majority of the songs were in English, many of which I hadn't heard in years, predominantly classic rock like Pink Floyd's "Another Brick in the Wall." We all joined in on the chorus: "We don't need no education... Hey, teachers, leave those kids alone..." The irony amused me. Though a stranger in a strange land, I found myself immersed in the songs of my high school experience, waxing nostalgic while trying to come up with the Turkish phrase for "where is the bathroom?" We arrived at home at four in the morning, dizzy from drink and decibels, and sweating anise from our pores.

Flopping onto the couches, we observed the disarray and munched-on breadsticks and cake, and guzzled water to avoid an unpleasant Sunday. Bob put on the Beatles' *Revolver* as we each nodded off where we sat, the words of McCartney and Lennon still on our lips... *I'm only sleeping...*

Kızılay

Not willing to let a moment go to waste, we rushed through the party cleanup the next morning so we could explore in the afternoon. Kızılay, the major commercial district at the center of the city, was a good half hour's walk through zigzagging streets, down Tunalı and then Atatürk Boulevard, Ankara's main thoroughfare. We passed tall office buildings, movie theaters and a McDonald's, which always takes a little of the foreign edge off of things. Inside buildings were plazas of shops, and a wide variety of restaurants and bars. Off the main streets, the smaller lanes closer to the center were actually closed to traffic (though some cars still managed to appear at our heels periodically).

We passed many kebap salons and *lahmacun* (a kind of meat pizza) joints. Plastic tables and chairs were set apart from the next establishment sometimes by a wrought iron fence or a brick wall covered in ivy or potted plants. The brick pavement was dirty and the smells were sometimes unpleasant. A man stood in the middle of the walkway with a grill and a box of meat and some corn on the cob. Unlike tourist areas, in Ankara no one accosted us to eat at a particular place. A man sold lottery tickets from a briefcase on what looked like a TV tray. He sat on a fruit crate and occasionally announced his presence to passersby. Another man spread out paperbacks on a sheet over the walk. The man next to him had posters— Ricky Martin, Che Guevara, Bob Marley, and a wiry man with short spiky hair and a pop icon look. Tarkan, we were told, arguably Turkey's biggest pop singer. ("Teacher! You like Tarkan?") His latest song, which we called the kissing song, featured a big smack at the end of each chorus and gave new meaning to the word "overplayed." Only Ricky Martin was as prominent.

Further along the street, we found Dost Bookstore, a well-lit establishment featuring an excellent English section. For me it was like a candy store. I came across various books still wrapped in plastic and approached the salesclerk, an attractive young woman with hazel eyes, long dark hair, and olive skin.

"Can I open this?"

Her smile was disarming, "Of course." She stepped behind a cash register and found a razor and carefully slit the packaging. "Where are you from?"

We exchanged a few pleasantries and I complimented her on her English, and she praised my meager Turkish. Her name was Havva, Eve in Turkish. She was studying tourism. I told her I would be happy to practice English with her if she would correct my Turkish. "I'm sure I will be here often." I hefted the book, "Thanks."

"It is no problem."

In an effort to make more headway into deciphering the language, the three of us purchased some Turkish versions of classics. I chose Hemingway's short stories in the hopes that his sparse style might make translation easier. I gave up in under thirty minutes.

We went to a nearby cinema, having heard that teachers received a discount. We simply said "teacher" and the lower price was given without questions. Movies were mostly in English with Turkish subtitles. It was an excellent way to pick up on colloquialisms while enjoying the show. I didn't know the language, but like Caliban, I was learning to curse in it. Part of the entertainment was to see a drama and take note of the places where the Turks laughed. Usually when someone was being sarcastic and grim, where I might think "Uh-oh, something bad is about to happen," they got in a good chuckle. The ushers actually ushered. All moviegoers were led to assigned seats that were handed out at the ticket window without any rhyme or reason. I hated this, since my seat of choice is second row—if I don't have to turn my head from left to right to read the credits, then I'm not close enough. Halfway back is out of the question. Once the film began, however, everyone moved to their preferred seats anyway.

About halfway through the movie I thought the projector had broken. The lights came up and everyone rushed out to the lobby and began smoking; a ten-minute intermission to switch reels accommodated the Turks' addiction to nicotine. Smoking is a national sport.

Outside the cinema was a long block of small shops like tiny garages, built of plywood and only large enough to shelter a couple of people from the rain. All of them sold books, primarily textbooks. Idle shopkeepers sat waiting for someone to buy something, hoping perhaps that somehow out of all these shops with identical fare, one of the handful of buyers would choose them.

We roamed around the last bars and restaurants that remained open. Traditional Turkish music was advertised but many places were already winding down. At night Kızılay takes on a stark quality. Garbage was hauled out from restaurants in torn bags and left lying in the center of the closed-off streets. Shopkeepers hosed down their storefronts and walkways and the runoff collected down the middle with the garbage. The smell of fresh fish from the open-air seafood displays was strong, and cats congregated everywhere, peering out from alleys and garbage dumpsters, darting between our passing feet, moving in shadows that continuously caught my eye and making me feel as if all the shadowy areas were themselves alive and moving with me, as my shadow had that afternoon.

In direct contrast, however, were the flower shops built along the center of one of the walkways. They consisted of tiny rooms constructed of plywood and window panes, and their bright and aromatic displays spilled out over the bricks. Bouquets and pails full of carnations, lilies, roses, and orchids took up three times as much room as there was floor space inside the shops. They remained lit up like Christmas with painfully bright bare bulbs that dangled from the awnings. It was the only thing to combat the gritty aspect of nighttime Kızılay.

But as we walked through the bitter air of the streets, we nevertheless had the sense that we were safe. There were no stumbling drunks, no suspicious looking characters loitering about, and the police seemed ubiquitous but not in an oppressive way. Officers sat reading papers or even sleeping in what looked like roomy telephone booths much like the one in our own neighborhood. Other officers passed in patrol cars with their lights perpetually flashing, occasionally yelling something through the loudspeaker of their radios. I still have no idea who they were yelling at: taxis cut in front of them, cars ran lights in front of them, people ran across the streets dodging buses and cars, yet nothing seemed to happen. But *something* would provoke them and suddenly garbled Turkish echoed off the buildings. Then they just kept driving.

In the Classroom

American teacher training didn't prepare me for the Turkish classroom. In the first few days I could see what I was up against. Education is by rote learning, and the emphasis is on math and sciences. By the end of high school, every student has studied some calculus, and I have heard it said that the average pupil can score near to perfect on an SAT math section. But put them in group situations for a higher thinking challenge, and all was lost. Yet this was the goal of our methods. My challenge was attempting to loosen up the limitations on their self-expression without doing the same for their self-control.

In the end I had to remember these were kids like any other kids. They wanted to run, they wanted to play, they did have thoughts they wanted to express, but each day they sat in sports jackets and ties, skirts and sweaters, listening to lectures. These teenagers, fearing the approaching university exam which essentially determines their futures, attended night classes. Conversational English class, then, was a tremendous relief; and, like a weak dam first springs a leak and then suddenly tears open, the force of all that pent-up energy was sudden and relentless.

Though I had to struggle to contain them, I never felt that darker, sarcastic and cynical bitterness which I often felt from many American students. Sincerity and respect, rare though not unheard of back in the States, was open and unabashed in my school. Popularity did not demand disrespect or defiance.

A sort of 1950s innocence prevailed, where the most radical offense might be a cigarette shared by the upper-class boys in the restroom. But all things must pass. In those older classes, the stresses of the impending exam, the weariness of night classes and the realization of the freedoms of youth never seen in generations past combined to wear away at that ingenuousness. I clung more firmly to my younger classes and fought against the tide even as I tried to teach them to look at the world critically and express themselves.

Each week I saw 225 students—six classes of sixth-graders, five of eighth-graders, one tenth grade and three prep classes. The *hazırlık* or prep classes were adorable and frustrating. Whenever I said, "Open your Cross Country books to page six" I'd get six of them rushing up to me out of their desks with books to show me. "Cross Country, *hocam?*—Cross Country?"

"Yes. Page six."

Another mob of kids, "Page six. Page six. *Hocam?* Page six?"

During break time, I avoided the lounge. I preferred to hang around the halls and practice with the kids—their English and my Turkish. The preps, with their programmed responses, were the funniest. "Hell-o teacher, how are you?"

"Good, thanks. And you?"

"Fine tanks, and you?"

"Good. And you?"

"Fine tanks…" It would go on forever if I answered again. I tried to go beyond the memorized responses.

"So, Mustafa, how was your weekend?"

His wide grin froze into his cheeks, but hesitation was clear in his eyes, which shifted back and forth as he attempted to process "weekend."

"Goodbye, teacher," and he ran off. When in doubt, say "See you."

Though the hardest to communicate with, the preps, compared to the other students, were the fondest of their teacher. By week two it became clear that Burak was one of the worst for bringing books up to me at the board; I turned around several times and tripped over him. For no particular reason, he brought me a kilo of roasted hazelnuts wrapped in Happy Birthday paper. Just a walk down the hallway was a series of snack offerings. Students would offer me their last bite. A chubby, blue-eyed boy named Menderes—his shirt untucked, a serious granny knot on his tie, and looking like he was exploding from his clothes—insisted I take his second candy bar.

The preps just sat there with anxiety-ridden smiles. They'd look around at each other and shake their heads no matter how slowly I spoke. But it was astounding how quickly they absorbed things. To avoid frustration, I had to remind myself: sixth-graders and a drastically different language. Imagine a class for an eleven-year-old taught completely in another language. In fact, they were amazing.

I wrote some sentences on the board for them.

"Teacher, teacher! Erase board?"

"How about writing it in your notebook first?"

"Yes, teacher, OK teacher. And den I erase board?"

As required, I had to send the lesson plan book to Chad before every period. Students fought over who would make the delivery. During one of my sixth-grade classes I had an idea to make this entertaining.

Bob, Chad and I had discovered we were all fans of the Simpsons. In fact, a couple of times since our arrival we had lain there in our separate rooms at night with the doors open, reminiscing classic episodes in the dark. "Hey. Remember the one when Bart—you aren't sleeping yet, are you?—the one where Bart tells Lisa that..."

I stood with the oversized planning book, thinking.

"Murat, can you tell Mr. Blair something when you give him the book? Tell him, 'Mmm, dooooonuts.'" He repeated it to himself, eyes rolled to the ceiling, and then raced out the door, his jacket tails flapping. Chad fired back with another line, and so it began. The kids groaned in jealousy. "Teacher, next time me!" I promised that we would follow a schedule for the opportunity to quickly memorize a phrase of nonsense.

I nearly laughed myself to tears the next day when Gizem, one of my smartest and sweetest, repeated (from the movie *Airplane*), "Bubba don't want no help, Bubba don't get no help. Ain't got no brain anyway." Later that day I stopped at the lunch line to pat her on the back and say hi. On the floor by her foot was a 25,000 lira coin, not worth the metal it was stamped on. "Ah, Gizem, look. You found a coin."

"No, teacher. That is not mine." What a doll. And she still could repeat that movie line suddenly standing straight as if it were a formal recitation.

Back in the classroom I dropped a pen; three kids leapt from their seats to retrieve it before I could even lean forward. Earlier in the week I had dropped the cap to my board marker and it had rolled under the video unit in the corner. Onur, a slim, spiky-haired sixth-grader, dove on his stomach like the winning run at the plate, feet waving around from underneath the TV as he struggled to find the cap.

I learned a few words to help me with the lesson and that little bit of Turkish met with applause and whistles. It was humbling in those moments of sudden reversal and I was the proud, beaming student facing his sixteen teachers. And for the students, that moment of being the experts must have been just as pleasurable.

One afternoon as we left school, passing among high fives through the students waiting for parents or buses, Chad stopped and bought some sunflower seeds from a street vendor. Across the street I saw Linda and another woman walking in the opposite direction. I shouted and stuck my arm up to wave and a *dolmuş* and two taxis screeched to a halt expectantly. Embarrassed, I withdrew my arm and hesitatingly the traffic moved on. We crossed the street carefully.

Linda introduced us to her companion. "This is Ceylan." So many of the Turkish women were beginning to make us feel like pathetic schoolboys and Ceylan was no exception. She had uncharacteristically short, medium-brown hair, and almond-shaped eyes with long lashes. Her father was American and she had gone to college in Texas, so her English was perfect. We chatted for a moment passing through the How-do-you-like-Turkey?-We-love-it routine. She mentioned that her husband was in town (our hopes sank) and perhaps she and Linda would go out for some live music.

Her husband, Türker, was completing his military service at that time and so was out of town frequently. All males were required to serve 18 months (it recently became 15 months). Going to university could only defer one's entrance, and though a degree did not diminish the requirement, it did allow graduates to serve at a higher rank. At the time, Turks could pay $8000 and serve one month. Clearly this deal did nothing for members of the lower class. Violent clashes in the East between the military and Kurdish rebels were more than enough reason to be deeply concerned about military service.

Near the bottom of the hill, the local police officer sat in a booth. His uniform featured a police patch shaped like the Grateful Dead emblem. He was reading the paper and listening to the radio, an automatic weapon laid across his lap. We waved, as usual; always a good idea to make friendly with the man with a gun. Chad stopped and offered him some sunflower seeds. The officer smiled and took a few in his hand and began cracking them in his teeth, then offered us ciga-

rettes. We chatted and he complimented us on that little
Turkish, as everyone did for any word or phrase. His name
was Hasan. We made some poor small talk of the weather.
"The day is beautiful." "Yes." "We are tired." "Goodbye"
(Stay happy). Every little bit felt like a victory and Hasan
became a regular part of my routine as I stopped there when-
ever he was on duty and at least asked him how he was. The
Turkish friendliness was intoxicating.

The Labyrinth of Ankara

One of the things I liked to do as a child was explore. In the small world of childhood, open backyards, crabapple trees, cluttered attics and garages were fascinating playgrounds for the senses. Part of my ambition in Turkey was to convert my everyday life to a similar richly textured fabric that could be touched daily. Suddenly, asking for olives at the market or giving directions to a taxi driver ceased to be a thoughtless reflex and became an engaging activity. And there still remained a whole new labyrinth of the mundane. Common streets and houses, pedestrians, and stray dogs—someone else's everyday scenery—were transformed into a sketchy treasure map marking the day's simple adventures.

The day we met Ceylan on our way home, Chad and I had to return to school a couple of hours later to meet with the parents of the sixth-graders. Linda led us around to several classrooms where she introduced us and translated our own introductory words to five rooms full of non-English-speaking mothers, stern-looking mothers, some with the traditional veils.

Conquering the anxiety of facing our silent audiences gave us a certain euphoria, and with that rush of energy we decided to go exploring. We had already been in just about every direction except toward the bottom of our hill. We looked off the edge of our neighborhood at streets that dropped away below the line of the horizon. Denser tree coverage and a lack of streetlights made it a black hole in the middle of the city.

Only a handful of lit spots represented neighborhood shops that huddled in groups of three or four.

The street wound slowly around the contour of what must have been a canyon before it was developed. I stopped for a can of sour cherry juice in a tiny grocery and watched a few minutes of a Turkish *futbol* match that had just started on TV. We walked in the dark street, unconcerned about nighttime safety but for the occasional taxi that veered past with a beeping inquiry as to whether we needed a lift.

We passed a small, unoccupied—and extremely rare— neighborhood park, a triangle between two merging streets, complete with a small patch of sand and three swings. Behind us a full amber moon eased into the sky, just above the dark outline of the sloping hill. Below it in terraced order, apartments came alive with lighted windows, and occasionally unseen televisions made the rooms flicker as though people were welding in their living rooms. Competing with the moon for the sky, a mosque and its two minarets with bands of white fluorescence stood like waiting rockets or space-age control towers.

Each row of apartment buildings was stacked flush atop the previous one. They became a wall of square lights that paved a way to the moon, the mosque, and the stars that competed with it all, and which were many despite the moon and a slight haze. Chad and I took it in silently before moving on.

But as we descended buildings looked older, smaller, and lacked the subtle touches of decorative gates or window gratings and the streets became sidewalkless and narrow. The smell of garbage and even sewage intensified, and the stink of animals joined the mix. A kitchen window or a streetlight choked by vines or unchecked trees provided meager illumination. Cars blinked their lights once as a warning as they squeezed by us between low buildings of rough concrete that pinched in close to the road. The houses were drafty looking, and some windows were uncovered, though I imagined (or hoped) that was simply for the season. An occasional sheep stirred behind fences of barbed wire or warped and rotted planks. Another car passed and we crowded to the side, snagging through branches that hung into our faces over a low wall. I put out my hand for balance and a gritty powder of crumbling masonry came away on my palm. I had a close-up look at the trademark red roofing tiles that sloped down to eye level.

Through open doors we saw families at wooden tables sitting down to meals in tiny kitchens amidst hanging laundry. Firewood lay in stacks alongside the houses. It wasn't quiet exactly, but the sounds were the subtle murmur of the simple life, not the raucous honking of taxicabs and the high whine of diesel engines and buses. I could hear the carefree laughter of children, something I always find most touching in areas such as these, places we would consider poverty-stricken, but only in material matters perhaps. "*Aah-naay!*" Like the two-syllable English equivalent "Mo-om!" that pleaded for a mother's response.

This was the village of Ankara. As in most countries with struggling economies, the jobs in Turkey are in the cities and draw the rural population. One wonders, however, if the pay-out outweighs the loss of open spaces, of knowing your neighbors, of safety, of the sense of home. But the country mouse doesn't cease to be the country mouse just by taking on a big city address — in many ways, in these poor neighborhoods, the spirit remains alive. Certainly the presence of farm animals was indicative of the dual nature of these dark streets, of a village within the city.

We came out into the light of an intersection full of shops—a kebap joint, a tea garden, and a market—and realized we were starting to get turned around. We headed back into the dark and crossed over a storm run-off channel.

Midway over the bridge, shots rang out—back and to the left, from somewhere up on the ridge. Not really close but within a kilometer. We looked at each other, nervous as rabbits, muscles taut and ready to run. "Naw." "Probably backfires." We chuckled nervously, both of us wondering how often backfires are so perfectly staccato and evenly-spaced. We walked a little faster. An American passport carries politics with it, and though most foreigners are quick to dismiss those politics in favor of the person standing before them, there are those stories of senseless overseas attacks that keep me careful.

"You know, Chad, no one would necessarily know we're not Turkish…" This was true; if we were in familiar territory, our comfortable demeanor generally allowed us to blend in. We both have dark hair and were still slightly tan from Fethiye, and the range of appearances in Turkey is much broader than I had expected. "…as long as we don't open our mouths anyway."

We started up another long hill and a lone, unhired taxi passed us. Still a bit nervous about the gunshots, I joked about my last thoughts on earth being "I *knew* we should have taken that cab!"

The trees rose up again and nicer houses lined the ridge to our left and stood level with us on the right, still deep in shadow. Ten minutes later, another barrage of "backfires." Six of them. Crisp and clear on the light breeze, and louder. Closer? I suspected the same source but perhaps our increasing altitude gave us a better earful. Seconds later there was a loud clattering up to our left, as if small objects were landing like hail on red roof tiles. Only a coincidence, I thought. Definitely close. We laughed in amazement—and perhaps in defense from fear—and picked up the pace. The next busy road couldn't be far off and the few passersby seemed unconcerned. We came out of the darkness and could look back and see the mosque, the moon a little higher in the sky. We began threading back around the upper edge of the "canyon" neighborhoods. We debated turns here and there and felt a growing confidence that we were on the right track. An ice cream shop made us hesitate.

I pulled out my pocket dictionary. It was often very difficult and exhausting to put phrases together, and at that point, we were tired enough to mull over whether we wanted ice cream that seriously. "I think we might be close," said Chad. My gaze wandered past him to the store two doors down. "Lights Market."

"Isn't that the name of the store outside school?" We looked at each other, then behind us, and there it was— Büyük Kolej.

We passed on the ice cream idea and began walking the last few blocks home. But just past Lights Market, we stopped at a low wall along the walk. Beyond it lay one of those rare empty lots sandwiched between buildings; it sloped away steeply—and dangerously if one fell off the sidewalk. A small boy passed us, leapt the corner of the wall, and let gravity lead his scurrying legs down a worn path. The other side of the block was less than a hundred feet away and we were able to see over the roofs of the four-story buildings there. The boy zipped through the wispy grass, hopped onto another wall alongside the building below, ran it like a balance beam, dismounted, and was gone. "Did you see that?"

We sat on the wall silently for another half hour looking down into the dark "canyon" and waiting with unfocused eyes for movements to draw our attention. A man stepped out onto his balcony for a few moments, a tiny cherry of fire glowing briefly at every drag from an invisible cigarette. A woman hung a sheet out on a line by her kitchen window. Two people argued in their living room, lit up in the sickly blue strobe of the television. A stone became a cat by moving to lick a paw beneath a large tree in the middle of the lot. This space was secluded in its own way, but right in the middle of our own backyard. Somehow it captured Ankara; framed by the wall, the buildings, and the stars, it was like a magic window opening out over the canyon and to the lights of the city beyond. We were to come back to this place often, after classes during the day or on walks in the evening.

Sated with images, we returned to the apartment. We flipped on the TV and scanned the three dozen cable channels, stopping for some *futbol* highlights—the match we had seen the start of at the market. The final score: 2-0. The goals had come about ten minutes apart, in the first half. We looked at each other, stunned. I did the math and figured out roughly what time we had heard the gunshots. We made an agreement not to leave shelter during important *futbol* matches.

Courting in Babel

"I love books. No. More than that. I love *words*."

She stares at me baffled. She repeats something close to what I just said but with different meaning, I can tell.

"No. *Words*. I love *words*."

The irony of the situation maddens me. We share no words. Nothing exists between us on the levels I am searching to connect on. Yet I am wrong. *Something* exists. I can't imagine what. Nothing romantic has happened. Nor would it, I think, without words. I sense she would consider wordless romance nonproductive. As would I. But there's something. A crinkle of frustration equal to mine emerges on her brow when I shake my head and mumble with heavy accent, "*Anlamıyorum* - I don't understand."

Her name is Sahil, meaning "the shore." Within days of school starting we have started to meet often and unofficially, by chance on her part, perhaps by unconscious will on my own. In the hall, across the lunch table, in the computer lab. I am like a hatchling; I have latched on to the first face I have seen in this new world. We exchange the series of Turkish greetings I've learned but deeper thoughts lie barricaded behind the bars of grammar and obscure vocabulary. Then we sit staring into our lunches, occasionally meeting in glances and smiles.

"Do you know what it means to love words?"

She laughs, shakes her long hair the color of eggplant. She reaches her hand out and holds my elbow gently, turning me a little as though to show me something or lead me on somewhere. But we remain where we're standing, motionless.

I sit next to her at a computer, and after repeating myself and looking to others in the room—students usually—for translation, I successfully ask her what she is doing. Something for her class. An exam perhaps. Something about the principal. Wearily, she puts out her lower lip and blows her hair out of her eyes. We stall again, smiling dumbly but warmly at least. I pull out a sheet of paper. "Write," I command her. A puzzled look. I hold up a pen.

"*Tamam mı?* OK?" I write a name. Kafka.

"Ah." She nods vigorously. She teaches German. I only know English and some Spanish. Four languages between us—none in common. She takes my dictionary and I interpret a subtle drop in her shoulder as, "Come closer a bit, not too much." I roll my chair next to hers. I can smell her hair. It smells like almonds. Her olive-colored fingers search through pages stained by the blackberries I bought from a veiled woman in the street yesterday. I want to tell her about that.

Linda later informed me that Sahil's Turkish was spoken with an accent. She had grown up in Germany. Berlin has the largest population of Turks outside of Turkey. Drawn by work opportunities, they formed Turkish neighborhoods and as the first waves of immigrants were primarily working class or rural people, they brought and sought to preserve a very traditional and often conservative culture. Now their children, born and raised in Germany, fluent in German and Turkish, were caught between the two, accepted by both but perhaps never fully part of either, living in a cultural limbo.

I hear her tongue clucking as she thinks.

"Ah." I read off the tip of her finger. Changed. To alter.

"Um. *The Metamorphosis?*" I guess.

She shrugs.

"*Tabii.*" Of course.

She laughs at my colloquialism. "*Tabii*," she repeats.

"Mm." Something occurs to her. Her hair falls across the paper as she bends to it. I wait. Hesse.

"Ah. Damien."

She squints.

"Never mind. Um. Steppenwolf."

"*Evet.*" She nods excitedly. "*Alman.*"

"German."

She says another word. I struggle for a moment or two until my dull ear hears author. "Ow-tor. Author?"

"*Evet.* Yes. Author."

I sigh an exaggerated sigh, wiping my forehead with the back of my hand. She touches my forearm with another easy laugh.

"America? Ow-tor? Author?"

"Um. Hemingway." I scribble, crossing out the extra 'm' I invariably put there. She sighs, puts a hand to her heart. A dreamy expression of raised eyebrows, sleepy eyes. She reaches for the pen. I feel her palm, warm and damp as I follow it away with my fingertips only for the merest fraction of a second. She glances at me, then the paper. Not a warning. Perhaps an acknowledgment.

She writes a sentence. I take the dictionary to my lap and this time she is behind me, her chin just over my shoulder, her arm crossing mine to pinpoint a definition.

What is my favorite?

I raise my eyebrows to say "Are you kidding? Can there be any doubt?" She leans away and turns her chair toward me expectantly. Her eyelids lift the merest bit.

"Gabriel Garcia Marquez."

She squints but smiles on, patient.

I write.

She reads. The way she mispronounces it—Mahr-kwez—is endearing. She repeats it melodramatically and laughs.

I look at her seriously and she softens some, waiting.

I write the title in English. *Love in the Time of Cholera*. She shrugs and taps the back of my hand with her finger. Suddenly light and nervous, I freeze. She points to the dictionary and I hastily turn to it. Write, she indicates. In Turkish, I understand.

I bite my lip. I write *Kolera*. Love. Um. *Sevi?* Time. *Zaman? Saat?* I cross it all out, shaking my head. She tears that piece from the paper and folds it once, thanking me. In the common Turkish gesture of something being first-rate, I signal 'delicious' by joining the tips of my fingers and my thumb and pulling them from a kiss. She mimics me. Laughs.

We sit silently. I feel off balance but taut like a loaded spring. I watch her eyes, the way the brown darkens around the edge of the iris from a reddish tint closer to her pupils. I am close enough to have to choose an eye. And I switch back and forth between them a couple times before looking away. My watch shows 5:00. The lab will close soon. She checks what she has been typing while I pack my book bag and rise to leave. I stop two steps off and turn back to her. I falter, conjugating verbs out loud.

To find. I find. *Bulmak. Bula... Buluyorum.* No. I bring. *Getirmek. Getiriyor...* I will bring, *getirecek... getireceğim.* Book, direct object, *kitabı*. Book I will bring, be bringing. You. *Seni.* No, *sana. To* you. To you book I will bring.

She cocks her head. Hesitates. I say good evening though I know she missed what I have said.

"*Hoşça kal.*" A Turkish goodbye. A command. Stay happy.

"*Güle güle.*" Go smiling. The reply.

The following day we sat together at lunch with Sahil's friend Mehrigül, a young counselor who spoke some English. I pieced together comments between mouthfuls, often consulting my pocket dictionary. Students entering the cafeteria saw me and stopped at my table to say *"Afiyet olsun,"* an equivalent of "Enjoy your meal" that could be expressed before, during, or directly after a meal. Each time Sahil smiled at me, emboldening me further. I invited her to play ping-pong when she said she liked the game, and after classes the next day we met downstairs. Mehrigül had come along but declined all invitations to play. I debated the ethics and cultural impact of letting her win. We bet for a coffee and I won in a close game. We agreed to meet at a nearby restaurant on Friday with Mehrigül after a teacher meeting.

It was time for another session of Ask Linda. "Linda? Is it me or is this woman afraid to be alone with me?"

"Well, if she's from a traditional family, and I'm sure she is, she won't be alone. It's kind of like a chaperone system."

And she was right. After a meeting on Friday it turned out that Sahil and I would be joined by Mehrigül and another friend. So I invited Chad and Bob as well. We sipped tea at a sidewalk cafe beneath the shade of a tree. Conversation stalled despite Mehrigül's attempts at translation and the affair was cut short when the women rose to leave.

"That didn't seem to go so well."

Chad patted me on the back and we headed for home.

From that point on, Sahil was still polite and friendly, but something had changed. The suddenness of it perplexed me. Perhaps it was simply the exhaustion of basic communication or perhaps I was too forward, not forward enough, needed a change of cologne, or should have never beaten her at ping-pong. Dating is complicated enough when on a familiar cultural playing field. This initial foray into flirting proved to be fruitless.

How to Cross the Street

Though Chad, Bob and I hadn't been living together long, there was a rhythm developing among us. Surely, there were great differences in our personalities. I was temperamental and headstrong, while Chad was a bit more thoughtful and level-headed. Bob burrowed through the world without flinching; he was the uncarved block. Things rarely got under his skin. A postcard stand could stop him for a half hour while I couldn't be bothered to see pictures of what I was about to or had already seen. All three of us were passionate music lovers. Though our tastes differed, we were enthusiastic to share a Turkish tune that had caught our fancy. We traveled well together and shared a childlike curiosity about our surroundings. When the opportunity to explore arose, we were ready to roll.

We had been trying to get a handle on the mass transit system. Buses at first were humbling. Sometimes when I got on, the driver demanded a ticket; other times I saw passengers pulling out coins. I had to step off a couple times embarrassed as the bus left me behind in a cloud of diesel. Another person waiting for a bus informed me that the red bus requires a ticket purchased at a special streetside stand while the blue bus accepts change. As for deciphering their routes, we simply boarded and rode them wherever they were going. Most of the buses passed through the center of the city anyway.

The *dolmuş* looked to be a convenient and cheap way to get around, but there were many different routes that overlapped and threaded their way through various corners of Ankara. It took us a while to ascertain which ones were going where and on that day we found ourselves behind the school, scrutinizing the signage on each passing *dolmuş*. In the front window of each was a destination name. But these were end points; if we were trying to find a stop before the end of the line, the signage would be no help. We wanted to go to Ulus, the neighborhood of the Citadel, to see one of the few Ankara sites in our guidebook—the Anatolian Civilizations Museum. None of the passing destinations were familiar names so we gave up on the *dolmuş* and took a taxi.

The driver had never heard of the museum but we used the guidebook to help him out. The driver's confusion and subsequent overzealous claim that he knew where he was going left me leery of our destination. How famous could it be if a local resident hadn't even heard of it?

The taxi ride, like most, was a hair-raising experience. We passed through optional red lights as the driver flicked his headlights. This might be effective at night but I wondered what purpose it served in broad daylight. He manipulated us through traffic, jostling us along the way. We were told that in an emergency a taxi was preferable to an ambulance: going in the opposite direction was an ambulance with flashing red lights caught in unreacting traffic. Stopped at another red light where we were turning right behind a long line of cars, the driver checked the oncoming lane, lurched into it, and raced to the front of the waiting traffic where he turned right in front of everyone else. My right leg began involuntarily twitching at an imaginary brake.

In the end the driver dropped us off breathless and giddy and at the wrong place. So we had to check a conveniently located "you are here" map to get our bearings and then head off in the direction we perceived to be correct. To do this we had to do some of what I call "portaging."

Portaging is leaving the relative safety of the sidewalk and crossing a major thoroughfare or intersection, which typically has no crossing lights. Or, if there are any present, they are ignored. You must time things precisely, stay alert at all times, and never fail to look in all directions. Look ahead for an indication that the flow may actually stop for a red light. Then get a good look at the eyes of the oncoming drivers as they slow down. Do those look like the eyes of a man who would purposely run another man down in the street, just to get another car length closer to his destination? Probably. But when he's stopped and has only a couple feet between him and the next car, your odds are good. So you rush into traffic with a hand out to your left. Just in case he lurches forward you can use that hand to launch yourself onto the hood. But the next lane is another story. Some cars may want to jump lanes, cars you thought were finally accepting their lot and waiting for the light to change. Often you cross the first lane and are forced to run against the flow to get around that car that just keeps creeping forward; you must at least make the two-foot-wide island before the light changes again or you are caught like a raccoon. There are no raccoons in Turkey, by the way. If they have such trouble crossing American roadways, they would have been wiped out at around the advent of the automobile here.

Buses create a serious hazard. One is stopped and you have two lanes beyond it to cross. You stand so very close to the front grill, where you can see the scratches and dents of cars or perhaps pedestrians who did not give the right of way. Is that a piece of torn cloth? But there is no time to examine. You peer around the corner and a Renault subcompact—yes, believe it or not Renault still makes cars and they seem to run—hurtles past your nose. The mirror will rip your arm off if you aren't careful. You have a problem. This lane is not backed up yet; the traffic is still moving there and the bus will soon be chomping at the bit. So you run left along the side of the bus, parallel with traffic, but facing it, not really certain where you will go if someone swerves. Then you duck across the lane only to run the opposite direction ahead of the bumper of a BMW. A BMW? Here? What's the insurance on THAT? He slows a bit so you can make some forward progress. The car you just passed behind swerves to the center lane and a taxi comes to a screeching halt and you leap past him as he blares the horn and makes gestures of anger that look like he's flinging his hand and can't quite remember which finger would insult you. This frustrates him.

So you've made the center strip and traffic starts again. You are stranded on an island in the stream. You are enveloped in diesel fumes. But for some reason there is a break in traffic coming from the right. If you are carrying anything you now switch hands, leaving the one closest to oncoming traffic open for a last resort catapult onto a car hood. You stagger your rhythm to get in front of the slower car in lane one and then slow to let the speed demon in lane two pass, and then you are one lane from the relative safety of the sidewalk; there is far less traffic on the sidewalk, though never nil exactly as drivers look for creative parking spots. You pause on the suggested dividing line for a lane (yeah, right) and wait for that final car—but wait! What's this? It is slowing. It stops. The driver waves you past. You stand staring, unsure what to do. A trick? Cruel joke? Cars behind him are honking wildly and at any moment they will be abandoning that lane and bearing down on you. The honking re-ignites your adrenaline and you make the curb just as the entire logjam of traffic explodes behind you. Ah, the adrenaline high. You are the king. You are alive. You are ready to grab life and suck the marrow from it. Grit your teeth and growl. Now get away from the curb before you get yourself killed by someone in search of a parking spot on the walk.

We continued on in search of the museum....

Ali and the Museum

A boy of about eleven hopped out of a barbershop looking as if he had some place to go, but I ran him down. "Excuse me. Where's the museum?" I asked him if he spoke English. He didn't. Then it looked like a language exercise. He let out a long sigh, looking back and forth at the street and shops behind me as though trying to determine the best route for a difficult journey. Something clicked and he beckoned us to follow. I expected him to get to the corner and point, but he continued, smiling the whole while. He asked me questions and I told him we were English teachers from America.

"Where in America?"

"Madison? Er. Milwaukee?" He squints. I sigh. "Chicago."

"Aaah, Chicago Bulls. Michael Jordan."

"Yeah. Chicago Bulls."

His name was Kaan and he led us through several turns, cut up a long set of concrete stairs and down some alleys. He was careful not to get too far ahead of us. We rounded a corner and headed up a steep, brick-paved street. He pointed. Just above us I saw the Turkish flag flying over the faded stones of the Citadel. Down from those walls is a winding road that follows a stone wall over which the sight of Ankara lies in its sprawling splendor. At the end of this road, before it empties into the anonymity of Ankara's repetitive streets, is the Anatolian Civilizations Museum. It was given the Best European Museum Award in 1997, though it is in the Asian part of Turkey. We shook Kaan's hand saying, *Memnun oldum*—pleased to have met you—and I slipped a 50,000-lira note into his palm. His eyes brightened but he immediately refused. I insisted. He refused once more. I grabbed his hand, placed the folded bill there and curled his fingers around it. He smiled broadly and wished us good day before rushing off.

The museum is situated in two Ottoman buildings originally built in the late 15th century. One part had been a *han*, an inn with a courtyard surrounded by two levels of overlooking rooms, the other a trading center for garments of pure Angora wool, from which Ankara takes its name. Everything is stone and marble with brick archways. We spent a couple of hours there, weaving through displays of pottery and artifacts dating back to the Paleolithic period, before 8000 BC. Turkey is part of the Fertile Crescent and is chockfull of artifacts and sites dating back to the first civilizations. Pieces from the kingdom of King Midas are on display as well as some pottery from ancient Troy. As I moved along from display to display, I walked five hundred years in three strides. From stone to pottery and then metals, and always more intricate. I passed through the kitchenware of everyday Phrygians and Hittites.

The inner hall was as engaging as the exhibits themselves. The arc of the ceiling slopes and turns into varying seams where the long flat stones come together and are supported by their own weight pushing down and together. Wide columns fashioned of mortared stones hold the roof over what had been a covered bazaar for the Ottomans. High above near the tops of the walls are tiny windows that let in the daylight. I tried to imagine its past: the floors covered with tables and baskets of produce, live and butchered animals, bales of lamb's wool; the perfectly square gray stones worn smooth by leather soles and strewn with straw and pistachio shells; the local sheikh with his lustful appetite and arbitrary temperament strolling through to have his hand kissed by the men and to cast lascivious glances at the women. But I am only speculating; there were no signs to read other than the blunt placard which informed me in poorly translated English that the building had undergone renovations and dated back to the Ottoman Empire.

I went and sat outside on a park bench. I was paging through my dictionary, looking up random words, when Ali found me. "Do you need some help?"

I looked up at the voice. "No, thank you, I am just practicing. Studying."

He sat with a sweater tied over his shoulders, eyeing me from the next park bench. "Are you English?"

"No, American."

He seemed surprised. "Traveling?"

"I am a teacher. I work in Ankara."

"Really?" More surprised.

We made some polite small talk and eventually I asked him to recommend a restaurant. Guidebooks be damned; locals usually had better ideas. He couldn't hear me very well and asked if he could sit with me on the bench. I responded with my new favorite Turkish word: *tabii*—of course. He smiled in a grandfatherly way.

Ali was a spry, seventy-year-old, retired elementary teacher who was working for the Ministry of Tourism as a museum guide. He took out his reading glasses to write the names of three restaurants on the back of one of his business cards. His hair was thick and steely gray, and like many Turkish men he had a beard of about three days. Shaving is not always a daily practice and is sometimes done three or four times a week depending on one's place in society: Bohemians and laborers, for example, typically don't spend much money on razors. He crossed his legs and threw his arm across the back of the bench. His voice was warm and confidential when he leaned toward me. His accent almost sounded French and he had a habit of saying "hm?" after statements to make questions. "You are a teacher, hm? You like Ankara, hm?"

Chad and Bob joined us and I made introductions. He suggested places to stay and where to buy souvenirs. He took out a map of Turkey from his book bag and pointed out some major historical sites in Anatolia. "This is the ancient Hittite capital city. You can go there, hm? Maybe you rent a car, hm?" He prodded the map in my hands with a stubby finger. "Here is natural spring. Kızılcahamam." I tried to repeat it quickly—Kuhz-uhl-jah-ha-mam—but he only laughed. "You will learn, hm?" He warned Bob not to buy books inside the museum as of course he had just done. "They are oh-ver priced," he said in a throaty whisper. "Do this. Your school has travel club, hm? The students, they travel, hm? Check with them. When they go to the Ministry of Tourism, you get a new map. The map here?" He leaned forward and wrinkled his nose in disgust. "Ohld. You want map? They give you one—" He leaned still closer, nodded, looked over his reading glasses: "—freeh... ohf... charge."

One of his restaurant recommendations was just down the street. As he was walking us out, another old man, also a guide, grabbed him by the elbow in a feeble rage. He babbled in broken English that they were on a rotation and worked for tips, and then sputtered a few other lines of outrage. He was dressed a bit sloppily and his crooked and rotted teeth gave him a shabbier appearance than Ali could ever have endured. Ali dismissed him with a vague wave as though absentmindedly shooing away an annoying insect. Years before they might have stood nose to nose, trembling, but now Ali barely gave him acknowledgement. "They are teachers. I am doing this freeh - ohf - charge. Go away. Ach!" The angry guide stood knitting his eyebrows and quivering his lips in a false start to protest.

Ali walked us out to the road to stand on the stone wall alongside it where it coiled down the hill, and we looked out over Ankara. The red rooftops were somber under gray clouds that had held back the rain as long as they could. Beyond the buildings, about a kilometer away, was a large expanse of green and a dull silver slate of water. "You see there, hm? There is Gençlik Park. It is big. You go there to buy things. Very cheap." Pointing to gaps between the rooftops below, he directed us to our restaurant. We shook hands, I took his card, and we descended back into Ulus.

We found the restaurant just as the sky began to lay a mist over the city. We walked into what might have passed for a greasy spoon in the United States, but the service in Turkish restaurants never let me think I was in a second-rate joint. There was always someone lurking about for the moment I finished a plate or glass (and sometimes before I finished it). It is considered an insult to leave a dirty plate before a patron. They were usually as smooth as quicksilver, and if you had a bite left, the waiter might be halfway to the kitchen before you could stop him. We ordered chicken kebaps, but the highlight was dessert.

It is called *künefe*. Composed of alternating layers of shredded wheat and a mild white cheese, it is soaked through with melted butter and is served hot with a generous coating of thin syrup. As we rose to pay the bill, my cheeks glowed and my stomach pushed at my belt.

Back in the street the mist had collected itself into a serious rain—not enough to clean the dirty pavement, but enough to make it slippery and muddy in spots, a hint of the forthcoming winter. The winter in Ankara would be considered mild by Wisconsin standards; temperatures never dip far below freezing and the snowfall is light at its worst. But the long afternoon of gray and drizzle and cold gave me a sense of despair. A full-blown winter at least has the magic of freshly fallen snow giving that illusion of purity. Winter in Ankara would simply be cold without an aesthetic payoff, long nights of barren windswept streets.

We were passing an intersection that had clogged with the traffic adjusting to the slippery conditions when I heard it—a horrible, bloodcurdling scream. I thought for sure that someone had finally met the Maker below the wheels of an unrelenting *dolmuş*. We all stopped in our tracks and turned towards the source. Sure enough, there it was again, and a *dolmuş* was backing awkwardly into an intersection. The victim sounded like a woman. I imagined severed limbs and a gory scene that would drag on forever while an ambulance attempted to breach the wall of traffic. But then I heard it again. A pause. Then again. Rhythmic, consistent, no variation in tone. The *dolmuş* stopped. Then it pulled forward. The screams stopped. I stood dumbfounded. "Was that the 'backing-up sound' of that *dolmuş?*" The *dolmuş* stopped again and reversed, making a y-turn. Amplified, agonizing screams. Up to that point I had heard a variety of horns and warning beepers. Some horns like a bugle's call to charge, at a volume that evokes an involuntary leap. Allah protect the man with a weak heart. I had also heard a couple of musical reverse-gear beepers. One was "Jingle Bells." This macabre creation struck me not as humorous, but foreboding.

We found a *dolmuş* back to Gaziosmanpaşa and I found standing room near the back. We gathered our coins and passed them forward through the other passengers like buying a hot dog at a baseball game. As usual the ride became seriously stuffed within a few blocks. Somewhere halfway home the driver began yelling something to all of us. Everyone standing around me maneuvered as best they could to sit on the floor. I followed suit, bewildered. After a block or two, everyone stood up. Bob had noticed that we had passed a roadside police station. No standing in *dolmuş*es allowed; at least not in plain sight of the police.

The *dolmuş* weaved, rocked, and surged forward into openings in traffic, and I watched the raindrops shudder and shimmy across the glass next to me. Beyond the drops I recognized storefronts from our neighborhood and soon our stop approached. I held my breath, rehearsing over and over in my head before blurting out at a precisely timed moment: "In-a-jek var!" meaning roughly, "there is someone who will step down." The *dolmuş* slowed a bit and we hopped to the curb even as it was pulling away. Wide sheets of rippling water slid down the road toward us as we ascended to our home.

The Simple Things

I found myself crowded into a raquetball court with about twenty people shouting to see who could echo the loudest. I had failed to come across as intimidating, because, frankly, I'm not. On Tuesday, the tenth-grade class was a scene out of "Welcome Back, Kotter," times ten. I had exhausted my short supply of crowd control skills and figured that perhaps three of the twenty-five students were actually listening. And they could hear only a fraction of what I said over the din of voices and in between confrontations. Then, already hoarse and disheartened, I met with 8E, the eighth-graders of the glued board marker. They knew they were smart, so anything I had to teach them was boring and pointless. Candan, a knowledgeable upstart with very good English, openly mocked me and loved to argue and complain of boring lessons. From there the class crumbled and I lost all control of them.

That day I was giving an exam and she chose to entertain herself by shouting answers to other students. I finally blew up and sent her out to her grade principal. This is a serious matter for them, and students typically come back reticent and remorseful or even teary-eyed after a serious Turkish tongue-lashing. She returned bitter but with evidence of having suffered a verbal beating. After class, I spoke with her for an infuriating twenty minutes of my lunch, during which she said it did not matter if she was sent out—her parents wouldn't care and neither did she. A haze hung over the rest of my day and the final classes were out of control and apathetic, an atmosphere more common on Fridays than on Tuesdays. I have always been one to take things personally, and for teaching the most important thing I needed was to develop a tougher skin.

But the simple things are sustaining. There isn't a day that goes by—in Turkey or back in Wisconsin—that doesn't present its own assortment of little magic moments. I stopped at Lights Market to guzzle down a Coke like it was whiskey and found Erdal leaning over the newspaper with a cigarette. When I asked him about *futbol* scores, he insisted I take the entire paper. Then I walked part of the way home with a student I met along the way who was very kind and reminded me that yesterday her class had been excellent.

I turned the corner on my street and leaned into the grade. I had my guitar with me and my school bag. My arms were tired, and my suit combined with the seasonable weather to add to my discomfort. I looked up then. Seven neighborhood kids, all five to seven years old, stopped what they were doing and stared. One of the boys ran up to another boy and whispered something, then they both ran down the hill toward me. "*Çantanız efendim?*" (Your bag, sir?) I could see them eyeing the guitar, but the way I was carrying it I think they estimated it was too heavy. So the boys grabbed my bag and I received an escort from the children of İzci Sokak. I was the strange man who lived upstairs and didn't speak the language. They were fascinated. (I was luckier than my great-grandmother, who spoke only Finnish when she immigrated to the United States; the neighbor kids threw apples at her!)

They led me up the stairs and waited patiently as I collected some mail and fumbled with the keys. I asked them in for Coca-Cola—wondering if I'd get any angry calls in Turkish about ruining dinner appetites—and they all began taking off their shoes just outside my door. I passed out the glasses and went along the line with a 2.5 liter bottle. One little girl, maybe five years old at best, said, "*Az*" - a little. I poured very little and asked her if she wanted more. Her little chin flicked up as did her eyebrows in the Turkish gesture for No: "Tsk." They inhaled the soda and had their shoes on before the little one could take a swallow. But she downed hers in two and was off, wrestling her feet back into her black patent leather shoes. How could I not smile?

So I looked at the mail. One for Bob, one for all three of us. Curious, I thought. I opened a wonderful letter from Veysel, the Kurdish student we had met in Fethiye the previous month. He was studying back in his "country," as he referred to the East. He was surprised and grateful that we had remembered him, and had been happy to receive the letter and pictures we had sent. Again we were invited to the East. I read his letter three times. His admiration for us— though perhaps a little overzealous—was flattering. I promised myself to write him again that week. It is a comfort for me to know that though people do cruel things for no apparent reason, there are many who have a kind deed for just as little.

The World's Most Popular Sport

Truly, one can't feel part of the male society in Turkey if he cannot answer what his favorite *futbol* team is. When students asked me questions my first week, most classes asked what my favorite team was before even asking me where I came from. The other topic of inquiry was:

"Are you marry, teacher?"

"No."

"Have girlfriend, teacher?"

"Um, no."

Then the mourning chorus of "Oh, teacher! Noooo!" As though they would all get up and hug me out of pity as if I were someone terminally ill.

But still they asked me: "Teacher, Galatasaray? Beşiktaş? Fenerbahçe?" Each student slapped his chest with pride when he spoke his team's name. It was time I picked. We received confirmation from several enthusiastic sixth-grade boys. "*Hocam, hocam,* my teacher! Sunday is match. Are you go to match, *hocam*?" On Saturday, a carefully phrased phone call from another sixth-grade boy provided us with the details. "Go to the stadium, take a taxi. Go early to the 19th of May Stadium." (Named after Youth Day, a holiday celebrating the future, first ordained by Atatürk. It is also Atatürk's adopted birthday. He never knew the actual date.) "Seats cost one million to five million lira." ($6-$30.) "You will stand in line. The game is at seven o'clock." Then he finished with the phrase common among Turks speaking English: "It is what you need." Their grasp of what we always needed was endearing.

The taxi driver let us off just inside the gates to a strange world within a strange land. As a lifelong Packers fan, suffering through the long years of losing teams and professional ineptitude, I know fan loyalty and enthusiasm firsthand. But *futbol* fanaticism is infamous, and this was my first glimpse of the sporting event that can send nations to war.

Police easily numbered 300 inside and out, many on horseback, wearing helmets with face shields and sporting battered nightsticks. I almost walked into the side of a horse in my stumbling amazement. Doors opened at 3:00 and though it was 2:15, a line was already wrapping around the stadium.

Vendors were everywhere, selling cans of soda and bottles of spring water floating in tubs of ice water, leaning over portable grills. Prices were fair—$1 kebaps and *çiğ köfte*, not the $5 beers or hot dogs one might expect for captive audiences in the United States. Fan paraphernalia from both teams was for sale, as were what looked like unassembled team-colored popcorn boxes. A man walked past carrying the legs of a TV tray and balancing a wooden platter on his head. He stopped, unfolded the legs, deftly set the platter down on it and pocketed a halo-shaped pad that made a flat surface of his pate. He offered a long curling tube of fried dough covered with syrup. I asked, *How much?* He indicated, *How much do you have?* I only revealed 50,000 lira in coins, which disappeared into his vest pocket. He drew a knife, cut a length of the inch-thick coil and skewered it on the blade. He folded a scrap of office paper around it. Later Bob bought the same amount from the same vendor with a 25,000 lira coin.

Police trucks, cycles, and cars still poured into the lot. A couple of white riot tanks complete with tear gas launchers backed into spots to await the outcome of the match. A man walking in front of us not watching where he was going was bumped by the side mirror of a Renault full of officers. The car stopped and the stranger stood hesitantly, mumbling, "Pardon." The officer stared at him coldly and spat out something in Turkish that didn't sound like an apology. Not one of them smiled. A boy, lingering next to his father's kebap stand, stood on an empty plastic water bottle, making it crackle and crumple under his foot. When he noticed a cop striding toward him, he stepped off, kicked it aside and took two nervous steps backward, closer to the stand. The officer passed on.

There were several lines and we chose the shorter line for the slightly pricier midfield seats. A man selling squares of inch-thick styrofoam to sit on indicated that we were in the right place. "Get rid of your change," he warned us. "They take it all at the gate so people do not throw it on the field." When I saw the change box and the officers filling it by the handful, I thought it seemed more like a fundraiser than a safety measure.

The ticket window was below my waist and I needed to crouch down on my haunches to see inside. Around the corner I handed the ticket to a man who inserted it in a computerized lock to open a revolving gate. Then we were frisked and searched by a cadre of twelve police officers before we entered the seating area.

The sun had come out and we looked down on more beautifully maintained grass than there was in the rest of Ankara. The fan sections and the playing field itself were separated from one another by high chain-link fences with barbed wire strung along the top. The seats—in the sections that had them and where they were not broken—were of white plastic, and we already regretted not having purchased styrofoam. Fortunately, there were enough old newspapers to put over some broken foam remnants from previous matches. It was not quite 4:00; the match wouldn't start until 7. We settled in and waited.

The sun hung over us in a mostly clear sky and we wilted under its intensity. The "popcorn boxes" I saw earlier turned out to be ill-shaped cardboard Galatasaray visor hats. My amusement turned to envy when the sun forced me to squint. I spent the rest of the wait with my jacket draped over my head like a veil.

Chad summoned a vendor toting a large burlap sack full of sunflower seeds. For a 50,000 lira bill he gave us a folded newspaper "cup" full of them. I had a few but decided that they were too much work, too little reward. I am a pistachio man. But it was fun for a while to try to spit the shells. By the end of the long wait, the guy in front of Chad had a modest number of sunflower shell splinters on the back of his shirt—much like our own shirttails. A cigarette vendor made me turn my head. The U.S. has really turned against smoking in public, so it was a small spectacle to me to look in through a bank window and see a teller lighting up on the job. Like many countries, Turkey has since followed the American example. But as the cigarette guy approached, everyone around us dug through their pockets to stock up for the match.

There was an opening game of noticeably amateur players. They wore Galatasaray (GS) and Gençlerbirliği (GC) colors, the day's professional matchup, and I think they were the Turkish *futbol* version of the minor league. The growing crowd watched halfheartedly and I became lulled into thinking that perhaps all the talk about the intensity was merely smoke. We sat impatiently, shifting as we became uncomfortable, and eventually I ventured down to the field level to purchase what passes in Turkey as a hot dog. Lamb's meat, I moaned. The size of the dogs resembled a couple fingers in a loaf of Italian bread with a bloody tomato sauce slopped over them—not comforting with the Chicago meatpacking stories in the back of my mind.

Back in my seat, I could feel the anticipation. The popcorn boxes were off and fans stood, though no one had come out onto the field as yet. Flags were unfurled, banners drawn out. I noticed a small platoon of riot police, complete with helmets, clubs, and plexiglass shields, standing at attention down on the field. They formed a line and proceeded to march around the track that encircled the playing field. Every forty feet or so, the last man stepped out of line and stood at attention facing the crowd. There were several angry-looking German Shepherds dragging officers around the track as well.

The riot control was serious business. A buffer of empty seats separated our seats from the Gençler fans. Police stood everywhere in sight—along the aisles, between the cheap seats and the opposing fans. They resembled prison guards with the chain-link and barbed-wire fences enclosing all of us. Everyone had that serious expression on the edge of a scowl like Hollywood's stereotypical Nazi storm troopers. But right in front of us, as the troops passed, a child yelled a name. The last man in line, looking ready for the Apocalypse, turned, smiled like Gomer Pyle, and waved. The crowd laughed and he stood in front of our section sneaking a wave from below the belt.

We had come to the match as Gençler fans. We were from Ankara, the home team, and to jump on the bandwagon of the previous year's champions, Galatasaray from Istanbul, just seemed wrong. But we were in "enemy" territory, the wrong fan section. We understood that we would NOT cheer openly. Though Ankara is the capital city, its teams were weak competition for Istanbul's clubs, and even though Gençler was the best of the three Ankara teams, we weren't very optimistic about the day's outcome.

Already the cheap seats on the GS side were boiling over.

Chants, songs and group motions made the entire end zone buckle and heave like a stormy red and yellow sea. We were sitting with people who seemed to be a bit more conservative: businessmen and their sons, older men, and—I counted— three women. There couldn't have been more than twelve in the entire place. Can we say "mega male-bonding"? For all their appearances, these fans were safe. But when the chants started, they all rose to their feet in response. It was the enthusiasm of a World Cup final, yet it was just another Sunday match against a second-rate team that barely mustered a home crowd.

Then the players came directly onto the turf through a tunnel under the stands and the track and up a covered stair- case behind the goal, far from even the strongest arm with a handful of coins, no doubt. When they appeared, the crowd went insane and drums started pounding. The answering cry from the Gençler fans was smaller but nonetheless impressive for such a meager bunch.

The teams warmed up on their respective halves. The GS fans would start chanting a player's name until that player jogged to the side of the field. He would wave, grin, and then throw an underarm punch three times before him, each punc- tuated by the crowd in unison - Oi! Oi! Oi! Well, here at least was something we could pronounce and we felt swept up in the enthusiasm, participating whenever possible though it wasn't our team. Hadji, they cried. Hadji is a familiar face. He figured prominently for Romania's run for the 1994 World Cup. He had resurfaced in the Turkish club scene.

The match itself was as exciting as being there in that strange world was. We were shocked and amazed when Gençler scored the first goal. Our whole section sat down with a collective curse. It wasn't long before Galatasaray was back in it, however. Everyone was jumping, slapping each other on the back, and twirling their GS flags. When Gençler scored again, I nearly became the sole voice to let out a yell in our section. Instead, we gave each other elbows when Gençler pulled ahead or tied the match.

At one point during the game a ball went out of bounds and one of the little ball boys stopped, frozen, with a snarling, leaping, but thankfully muzzled dog between him and the ball. They played with a second ball and he did not retrieve the original until the dog was gone.

The energy of the crowd surged right into the second half. The drums were pounding like going to war. I looked up at the stars. From where I was sitting, the sky seemed to honor the moon and star of the Turkish flag. Across the field, above the press boxes rose the crescent moon, thin, crisp, and bright, and Venus, too, was on the rise; it pierced the sky, shaming the constellations. In the distance, Atatürk's mausoleum stood proud in spotlights, a centerpiece on Ankara's table. From our seats we could look back at our neighborhood up on the hill a couple miles away.

When my eyes returned to the match I noticed how hazy the view was despite a clear sky. I looked around for a bonfire but found only—cigarette smoke? There was no breeze to speak of and the bowl shape of the stadium collected the exhalations of 30,000 people or so. It amounted to the equivalent of a light fog. I could hardly believe it, but as I watched the smoke curl away from the people around me I could find no other explanation. And there were the vendors, of course, to keep that fire lit.

The last minutes of the game were very tense. Gençler had scored their fourth goal and Galatasaray seemed to be moving the ball desperately and sloppily in attempts to add another to their three. There were some close calls and we waited anxiously until the referee blew his whistle. A roar of disgust from the GS fans. Squares of styrofoam went whirling through the air toward the bottom of the stands. Good thing they didn't have pocket change.

We hurried our way to the exit, the crowd pushing at our backs, and I wondered about those times when people get trampled at concerts. Then something odd happened. The GS fans around us started chanting: "Gençler! Gençler!" I am not sure if it was out of respect for an opponent or out of sympathy for the home team they weren't faithful to, but it was a comforting end to an event that had seemed so potentially volatile.

Outside, the crowd was orderly and my concern about getting a taxi was unwarranted. There were several waiting and the bulk of the crowd was climbing aboard buses and *dolmuş*es. We returned to our flat with the enthusiasm of children returning to school after Christmas to talk about what we had seen, what each of us had noticed.

Pay Day and Kiss the Teacher

Monday I returned from school with an envelope full of cash. Half of our pay came in Turkish lira, the rest in U.S. dollars. $600 worth of Turkish lira was over 100 million. The largest bill at that time was the 5-million note, and it was often very difficult to find someone who could make change. Taxi drivers would groan and stop at wayside stores, searching out smaller bills. But the amusement of being a "millionaire" wore off fast. During the school year the three smallest coins became obsolete and a 10-million note was on the horizon. Inflation was noticeable as the lira slipped fast against the dollar. On pay day everyone exchanged TL for the stable USD. [In 2005 the large numbers were phased out for new Turkish lira, dropping all six zeros.]

That afternoon I had stopped with Chad at Hasan the police officer's little booth to say hello. After the simple exchange of greetings and weather and a little attempt at sports talk, Hasan asked us something but we didn't recognize the word. He held up his little finger and made a slashing gesture with the other hand across it, then pointed at us with a sort of shrug and look of expectation that indicated it was an interrogative. We shook our heads and I fumbled with my pocket dictionary. I asked him to repeat the word. Turkish spelling at least was easy; one letter for one sound. "Just a second, just a second...." I followed my finger down the page, and he leaned over to see. I found the word. "Ah. Er... 'circumcise.'" Turks weren't generally shy about being curious.

Their interest in foreigners is unabashed and they often test what they think they know, from TV or Hollywood, against what a traveler can tell them. Hasan was surprised to find that circumcision was common in the West, independent of religion. You don't have to travel halfway around the world to find out something new about it. Just be curious and ask questions.

Now that we had cash rolling in, Linda suggested we hire a cleaning woman. She contacted the *kapıcı* and we settled on a modest price for her to come every week or two and give the apartment a good cleaning and wash some laundry. She even did the ironing.

A *kapıcı*, literally 'door person,' is a sort of building caretaker in apartment buildings. Our *kapıcı* was technically the man who lived in the basement apartment. The small yard and its rose bushes, the mopping of the stairwell and general building maintenance were all his responsibility. In winter when the coal comes in a great pile by the roadside, it is his job to restock the supply in the basement and maintain the building heat. But as I saw it, our *kapıcı* was Elif, his wife. Her husband was never around and she did everything, while taking care of her two sweet children, a girl, Canan, and a boy, Burak, about nine and eight respectively, each with large, liquid brown eyes and a certain timid kindness.

Elif herself was quiet and serious, but quick to smile when I said hello. But she was not a timid person, as we saw the time the yogurt man had come to call and she had dispatched him posthaste. She was a comfort to have around, and we were very happy with our arrangement.

The next day classes were shortened for a student presentation. In the gymnasium a dozen sixth-grade girls put on a dance routine. To the Latin beat of a Ricky Martin song, the girls gyrated and undulated like women in MTV videos, and it seemed a bit inappropriate. But a Turkish teacher leaned over to me without taking her eyes from them, saying, "Aren't they sweet?" *Sweet?* I thought. At the moment it merely seemed awkward.

In the States, there is a well-founded paranoia about being alone or having even the most innocent physical contact with a student. The rule was "cover your ass." Don't close the door, don't be alone. An American tragedy I say, and I admit that the open affection of the Turks was an awkward adjustment for me. I tried to explain this difference to the Turkish teachers and they were baffled. It was natural to hug children, natural to receive and give kisses on the cheek. But in the U.S. we sexualize affection, perhaps because of our TV shows and from omnipresent stories in the news about child molesters and sexual harassment.

Later I stood trying to chat with Ebru Dark between classes. The hall was its typical ten-minute reenactment of storming Normandy. Race to the playground, shoot a few buckets, race to the class, scream bloody murder. One of my sixth-grade girls came up to me in the hall and said something I didn't hear.

"I'm sorry, what?" She repeated but I still couldn't hear her. "One more time?"

"Teacher, may I kiss you?"

Big blush. "Er... um... we... uh. *What??*"

I received a simple peck on the cheek and though I was befuddled by it all, Ebru Dark only smiled. I had been warned to expect it but I must admit I felt silly. Some of the kids were aware of that cultural difference and so until it was established that kissing the teacher was legit, they asked first. Weeks later the idea was returned to innocence. My favorite class 6F had had an excellent day; they behaved, we had fun, and they did great on an exam. At the end of class, I went to the door to open it for them, and when I turned, I found them all lined up—all sixteen of them—waiting their turns to give me a peck on both cheeks. "Tank you teacher. Have a nice lesson."

Their adoration was a counterpoint to my daily combat with chaos. The next day, finally giving in to my resistance to raising my voice, I began to yell at classes when they had great difficulty staying in their desks and talked nonstop through the lesson. Afterwards they hugged me! "Sorry teacher. Next week we are better." Ah, the promises of children. Two minutes later the chatter of Turkish skitters off the cement walls and makes my head ring.

Talking Islam

A couple days later, during my break I went down to the snack counter for a candy bar. The students crowded against the counter like a mob rushing the vendor, crying "*Abi! Abi! I want...*" *Abi* means big brother and I had heard adult men say it to older men in passing as well. They said *abla*, big sister, to the female custodians. Once at a restaurant the waiter had spoken in reference to me to the Turkish woman I was dining with, "And for our brother-in-law?" Literally or figuratively, everyone's family in Turkey.

I went back upstairs to tell İffet of the previous evening's adventure as I routinely did, like a boy returning home to talk to his mother about a good day at school. When it was a simple story, I would try to do it in Turkish. She'd listen with amazement as I rattled off a list of mundane activities in Turkish: "...and then I got up, and then I brushed my teeth, and then I went to the store and bought some eggs, and then...." Then she'd turn to other teachers in the office, "Come listen to this!" My finger painting was being mounted on the fridge door.

When I entered the office I kissed the back of her hand and touched it to my forehead. "Ahh!" She laughed. "Where did you learn that?" It was something I had seen in the street. "You only do that to old people as a sign of respect; I am not old!"

But as I told her about the previous night, her smile stiffened with contained anxiety for her three grown children who were accepting candy from strangers, fortunately this time without razors or poisons. She sighed and gave me a "What am I to do with you" face. "You must be careful, you know."

The night before we had hopped a *dolmuş* down to Kızılay to visit Dost bookstore. I looked through the new English arrivals for a while and then struck up conversation with Havva, the bookseller. She looked ill with sadness. I asked her why and she explained that her brother, who had been doing his military service, had died just weeks before in an ambush in the southeast. War never makes a real impact until it comes off the television and into our lives. I expressed my heartfelt condolences, still unclear of the intentions of either side of the fight.

Not far from the store we stumbled across a demonstration in the street. We stood on the walk opposite trying to determine what the issue was. I asked a man with a briefcase standing nearby wearing nice pants, a tie, and button-down shirt. He told me the obvious: it was a protest.

The police showed up but stood by patient and relaxed. The crowd's energy was stable and when they began to disband, the man turned his attention to us.

Mustafa was a "political" writer, he told us. He withdrew a newsletter in Turkish to prove it. "I can show you my office. It is very near."

We rounded a corner and entered one of many indistinct apartment buildings. We stepped into a small elevator with an iron gate and emerged in front of a fourth-floor apartment. The door opened and an unshaven man with dark brown hair offered a gentle nod and firm handshake to each of us.

The apartment smelled of foot odor. All along the carpet by the door were an assortment of old shoes like the entrance to a mosque. We added ours to the collection and entered the living room where we were greeted by nine men in an atmosphere that suggested a prayer meeting.

We were instantly center stage. No sooner had we gone through the "Where-are-you-from? -work? -like Turkey?"

routine, than they divided into three groups, each one addressing one of us and investigating our religious beliefs. Unfortunately, like far too many of the people who are interested in what you believe and why, they were really interested in telling us what *they* professed, and why we must too.

For all our time in Turkey up to that point, our experience with religion had been limited to hearing the five daily calls to prayer, which with time were simply becoming part of the atmosphere, like a church bell back home. Back in school, religion was a required class for all Turkish students who were Muslim. Yet despite the fact that 99% of them are, there is no form of school prayer, nor religious representation in *any* school, public or private. The only exception were the schools for students aspiring to be imams, Muslim prayer leaders. Despite the homogeneous faith, Atatürk had known that a religious state could only lead to problems and the laws were made accordingly. Separation of mosque and state—despite constant political movements by religious parties to make it otherwise—is an important aspect of Turkish government.

Bob, a Protestant, went along with the topic defensively and held serious debate with his group regarding his thoughts. Chad, a professed atheist, defended his position while I, more of a Catholic-turned-neutral and terribly opinionated, thought it better to divert the conversation to the irrelevant.

One man began with me in almost nonfunctional English by taking the strategy of first acknowledging the validity of Christianity: Jesus as prophet accepted by Islam. He even drew on paper to help me follow. "Jesus, yes, good. He is prophet. But Jesus—finish!" He slapped his hands across each other like dusty work had been completed. "Now, Mohammed. Jesus" (slap, slap) "finish."

His name was Ishmael, a popular Turkish name, and I smiled at it. "Ah yes! I know that name."

"In Bible."

"Yes, yes, and he is a famous literary character. Er... in a book. *Kitap?* A novel. *Roman?* Um... Moby Dick. You know, literature?" To his bewildered look I set into a Pictionary session trying to describe the White Whale and the narrator who shared this man's name. My relentless attempt to convey this, including a rather crude drawing of a whale, left him somewhat unsure of how to return to his proselytizing.

Our host brought out platters of Turkish confections and, as we were in Turkey, we were served tea, traditional and apple. Chad chose the apple tea, a popular option—but not for Turks—that I never grew fond of. We sipped tea and melted sugary treats on our tongues, as Mustafa explained the group. Their intentions (they meant as part of a larger movement) were peaceful. They didn't want to *control* the government but to make the truth public, to *guide* it as it were. We smiled politely, nodded at times. Like some of my own culture's converters, I thought. But then again, no: *I* had sought *them* out, not vice versa. No one had nor would come to our door to speak to me about Allah. It made the Christians trying to convert fellow Christians back home seem even more zealous.

The hour was getting late and we took our leave of them. They invited us to come back any time to discuss things and we waved through the iron gate as the elevator took us back to the street. "Well, that was interesting," said Bob.

"Yeah, but İffet and Linda are going to think we're nuts to have gone in there."

We made for the central park to find a ride. The air held a chill, and a scratchiness in my throat told me I had a cold coming on. The weather was changing. In the park, hailing a taxi for home, we heard the final call to prayer sounding across the city. The night's events had made it once again an object of fascination.

Istanbul, Not Constantinople

I spoke to Can briefly on a pay phone; he was on his way. We stood at the bus station outside the city and I worried that I wouldn't recognize him since I had only spent that original flight with him. Chad and Bob had met Can only long enough to shake his hand. So I was relieved when a compact Toyota pulled into the lot and someone waved to us. I had no sooner waved back when he was out and around the car, embracing me like a lost brother. "Welcome to Istanbul!"

I reintroduced Chad and Bob and we loaded our bags into his trunk.

"Are you ill?" he asked.

"Yes," I answered.

"*Geçmiş olsun.*" ("May it pass." It can also be applied to *futbol* losses and bad test grades.)

Can drove us along the narrow strait known as the Bosphorus, also called Boğaz (the Throat), which divides Istanbul as well as two continents, and connects the Black Sea to the Sea of Marmara and, further on, the Aegean and Mediterranean. We were in Asia, south of the city, and we went in search of a bar. Istanbul, with over twelve million people, is spread out. Without a car, the taxi rides would have become expensive.

We were turned away at several clubs. Can explained, "It is difficult for men. Clubs will not let them in without women. Men drink and fight sometimes about the women. For this reason." After an hour, we found a low-key sit-down sort of place and Can convinced the doorman to let us in. Hardly any people were inside and at this point the only thing the bar was protecting itself from by turning away men was making money. We ordered beers and the waiter brought out a basket of peanuts which we all began methodically dismantling. Moments later, the power went out. We sat in the dark and the sudden silence up and down the street, but then candles were lit and everyone resumed activities without concern.

"Are you hungry?"

We said Yes in unison, having kept this knowledge to ourselves out of some perverse form of politeness.

"I know a restaurant. Do you know *işkembe*? It is what you need."

As it turned out, *işkembe*, a popular tripe soup, was not what I needed, nor will it ever be. A rumored preventative medicine for hangovers, it makes me shudder. Fortunately, they also had my favorite meal, *mantı*, the ravioli-like dish smothered with yogurt and garlic in oil. Though the air was brisk we sat outside where the faint fishy smell meant we were finally at the sea again. I loved Ankara, but ask Turks what is missing there and they will tell you: *deniz yok*. No sea.

A few leaves skittered along the sidewalk and I noted that the changes of fall were subtle and the leaves only yellowed a bit before twirling to the ground. Trees were relatively few in Ankara, as were the fiery autumn colors of Wisconsin. A few weeks after this trip, in a moment of casual absurdity, I saw a man, a rake over his head, scratching at the scrawny tree in his small yard to hasten the handful of leaves on their journey.

Our increasingly frequent yawns emboldened Can, who had been stifling his own, to suggest we call it a night. We tumbled into his car and he helped us check in at a hotel, insisting we call him the next night to go to dinner.

The next day, our tour guide was Erkan, the young man we had met in Fethiye. In two days two people we had met before—only for a few hours and in different contexts—were making good on their offers to hook up with us almost two months later and show us around. As an American, I find too many people, including myself from time to time, express invitations or wishes that are never meant to be taken seriously. It was refreshing to experience them in all sincerity.

We waited for Erkan in front of our hotel near the ferry landing. He suddenly appeared standing next to us wearing dark sunglasses as though he were trying to be inconspicuous about meeting us. He was looking around us and initially didn't even smile. "Follow me," he commanded and we rushed off to the ferry.

What followed was a whirlwind tour of Old Istanbul. The ferry took us up the Bosphorus, the sole channel out of the Black Sea, which sees a lot of sea traffic. We passed many container ships, other ferries and an assortment of tiny fishing boats that tipped and swayed radically in our wake while their occupants seemed barely to notice. Our ferry followed the Asian coastline north and then cut across the open water to the Golden Horn—a long inlet and natural harbor that cuts into the European side of the old city with its kingdoms stacked upon empires. Byzantines once kept a chain across the water to keep out warships. Mehmet the Conqueror led the Turks as they carried their ships overland to take the harbor. On both sides, magnificent domes and minarets rose out of the skyline tinged blue with a haze. As we disembarked on the eastern side of the Golden Horn, a cloud of seagulls flying in a frenzy over the bounty of the fishing boats became an aerial threat. My jacket received a direct hit. Erkan smiled, "Ah, in Turkey this means good luck." A rather optimistic Turkish belief.

We crossed west on a bridge full of vendors selling drinks that cooked in the sun, fresh (hopefully) mussels and lemon wedges, and clothing spread out on tarps along the walk.

Dozens of people fished with long poles slung over the railing. Foot traffic was as congested as the cars and trucks.

On the other side we ascended curving streets to the oldest section of the city. Erkan told so many stories that I had to ask him how he knew so much. The answer explained his good English as well. As a child, growing up in Istanbul, he had hung around the historical sites. He listened to foreigners and guides, accumulating enough knowledge and confidence until he was ready to offer free commentary to anyone willing to let him practice his English.

And so we whirled through history. Roman Emperor Constantine gave the city his name—Constantinople—in the fourth century, but before that it was Byzantium, which would later become the name of a Christian Empire that stretched into Anatolia. It is one of the most frequently besieged cities in history—understandable, as it lies at the crossroads of continents and controls a seaway. The Turks had always called it Istanbul, which became its official name in 1930.

Our first stop was Topkapı—literally Gate of the Cannon—the former palace of the sultans. Situated on the upper slope of a hill, it looks out over the waters of the Bosphorus. It took a long time, even in our hurrying, to see all the rooms filled with majestic treasures. We stared in wonder at a bejeweled dagger in a glass case, a treasure that was the centerpiece of an old Peter Ustinov movie also called *Topkapi.* I was stopped short by what looked like a golden arm. At the back of the hand I could see human bones through a square cut in the armor. The display read: "The forearm of St. John the Baptist." I wondered aloud where the rest of him was. (Later I found his alleged tomb in Damascus, Syria, and wondered if he lay inside, sans arm. Had he been buried with his head?)

We enjoyed Cokes under the trees of the center courtyard

and then ventured back out the main gate to the jewel of the Byzantine Empire, Hagia Sophia, or Ayasofya as the Turks call it. Originally a basilica commissioned by Emperor Justinian and completed in 537 AD, it became a mosque at the fall of the Byzantine Empire when the Turks invaded what was then Constantinople in 1453. Since a proclamation by Atatürk in 1935, however, it has been a museum, a symbol of the layers of Turkey's religious history wisely given a neutral secular commission.

Between our rushings about were the pauses where we lay on cold marble or leaned on banisters to stare at magnificence. The massive space beneath the main dome and its half domes of equal magnitude was dizzying. Considering the absence of modern construction convenience, and the fact that it was built in earthquake-prone Istanbul, its survival is nothing short of miraculous. The 105-foot diameter dome rises up 184 feet and appears to defy gravity. Absent are the massive columns that typically support the edges of a dome so enormous. It rests instead on two half domes of equal size. Christian mosaics, glowing with a golden sparkle as though from an invisible light source, share the space with giant medallions with Muslim calligraphy. Even the invading Muslims, who forbid representations of God and people, found its beauty overwhelming. According to Erkan, Mehmet the Conqueror said that anything so beautiful could only come from God. So rather than destroying the icons, they covered them with plaster. Some are still waiting to be restored.

Moving us along, Erkan took us back into the harsh sunlight. From Ayasofya we looked out across a park with a large fountain as its center point. Through the mist and rainbow that it cast toward the skies, we could see Sultanahmet, the Blue Mosque, the Turks' reply to Justinian's dream. Six minarets stood sentinel to its massive dome and surrounding smaller domes. We took off our shoes as is required to enter a mosque. The main prayer area was sectioned off by a wooden banister. The walls and ceiling were decorated with blue ceramic Iznik tiles, and the colored glass of the towering windows helped create the ambiance appropriate to a holy place. Tourists seemed a bit too loud, however, and I found it a wonder we were allowed in at all despite our stocking feet and the hastily covered hair of female travelers. Again we soaked up what we could of the place before Erkan kept us on our schedule.

As we passed through the gate to the street again, Erkan, in tour-guide form, directed our attention to the minarets. At their completion, the Sultan received some heat from Mecca, the center of Islam, where the central mosque also sported six minarets. As this was interpreted as an attempt to upstage, and an act of pride, the Sultan was forced to finance a seventh minaret far away in Arabia to keep the peace.

Erkan scuttled us past two obelisks and then on to Yerebatan Sarayı. From the street just across from the corner of Ayasofya, we entered a small nondescript stone building that resembled a guard station. Inside we entered a stairwell that descended into damp air. At the bottom, an underground world opened up to us. We stood in a cistern of the Byzantine water system. Columns stretched out in the dim light provided by a few colored bulbs throughout the cistern. A walkway circled the center and extended to the far reaches, where we found two special columns that were supported by large stone heads of Medusa. The echoing drips sent out ripples toward us from the dark corners and the cool air was a relief from the heat above.

Outside the sun was sinking fast. We bought bread, olives and soda at a market, but we needed to move quickly once again if we were to get to another famous mosque before the call to prayer when it closed to tourists. The mosque of

Süleyman the Magnificent is the largest in Istanbul and after admiring the glow of the lights inside and the rich colors of the walls and the ornate rugs covering the floor, we stepped back into the courtyard to pass the test of the Sultan. Erkan took us to one of the massive surrounding pillars and showed us two depressions on either side of it in the marble platform that bordered the courtyard at knee height. This, as the legends of Erkan told us, is where a soldier's agility was tested. If he could step in one depression with his left foot, and then cross before the column with his back to it while stepping with his right foot (without falling off the platform), he was worthy. The curve of the column pushed at our backs as each of us struggled to bring a right foot into the opposite depression before falling. None of us left until we were worthy. Then we sat with our food behind the mosque in a yard full of grass and waited for the voice of the muezzin. We enjoyed a simple feast as the call to the faithful rang out over our heads, bringing a satisfying end to a tiring tour. I was later to find that this little picnic hinted at a class system that was about to rear its ugly head a bit.

Later that night we met Can and Erkan in Taksim, a commercial district filled with shops, clubs, and some good seafood restaurants. Down İstiklal Avenue—which, though blocked to traffic, still had the occasional car that sent the crowds to the sides—we encountered a protest. Being from the Midwest, my experience with crowds speaking their collective opinion was limited to the occasional picket lines of worker strikes. Here people seemed much more politically-minded than back home. We didn't know their cause and something simmering in the chant kept us from approaching the perimeter to inquire.

Erkan arrived first and we waited at the top of the avenue for Can. We introduced him to Erkan but something seemed amiss. They greeted each other with a formal stiffness, but it was gone in a moment and we moved on. Can took us to a gallery that contained nothing but seafood restaurants. Tables and chairs lined the passageway and to either side was a different restaurant every ten paces. I wondered how they sorted out the competition, and for that matter, which of the scattered tables and their customers belonged to which establishment. Using some method of divination that I wasn't privy to, Can determined the best place. The owner, a robust old man, ran through the fresh selection in a refrigerated deli counter at the door. Can asked us a series of questions about likes and dislikes and then the host said he would take care of it. There was something unsettling about it, as though Can were the most powerful and feared man in the neighborhood and a regular, though he had never eaten there before.

Erkan was notably quiet and even seemed to squirm a bit. Can wolfed down a plate of mussels stuffed with spiced rice. Succulent food came out in rounds, and all was accompanied by our *rakı* laughter and the sound of a robust old man wandering the tables making a silver clarinet sing.

After the meal we stood in the street unsure of what to do next. Can and Erkan discussed the matter tersely and the tone suggested there was disagreement. Erkan seemed to give in quickly without making eye contact with Can, and Can led us on with a restored smile. The previous night's problem of not having dates resurfaced. We ended up in a smoky bar that blared Turkish rock. The crowd was entirely men and only a stumbling few danced halfheartedly by themselves. My first thought was that this was a gay bar but the listless demeanor of the patrons and the grunginess convinced me they were simply men who couldn't get dates. We sat in a corner, unable to talk over the volume, five men staring morosely into their warm beers until we called it a night. The next day we purchased our return tickets to Ankara from a bus company near the hotel and boarded the five-hour ride home.

Over the following months I pondered the situation between our two guides. Can was a pilot, from a well-to-do family—Erkan, a self-taught man who had made it to the university from public schooling and who held a small banking position. A comment Can had made the first night at our hotel regarding the manager stuck out: "Careful. He is Anatolian," meaning he was uncouth or prone to anger. The idea was that this was a result of his rural origins and suggested that he was from the East, possibly Kurdish. To be fair, of course, there is a significant difference in cultures between the city folk and the massive wave of villagers who immigrate to Istanbul in search of work. Whether or not this sentiment is what tainted the relationship between Can and Erkan, I may never know. But it became clear to me that Can would never have picnicked outside a mosque in Istanbul, and Erkan would have led us to a less glitzy restaurant and a different neighborhood altogether for a beer.

Location, Location, Location

With each passing day my love for Turkey grew while my despair with my classroom followed with it. My teaching felt more and more like crowd control. Each moment of frustration was followed by some sort of small reminder of how much the students liked us. This meant pleasant greetings, hugs, high fives, or an occasional broken-off share of a candy bar. Despite my culturally biased view of the school as lacking effective discipline, Büyük Kolej was a reputable establishment. Graduates did well on the university entrance exams that are required for all higher education, public or private. And Linda made sure we understood how fortunate we were to be teaching at a private school.

Public schools were free but were part of such a chaotic, overcrowded system that if one wanted to go to the university, the odds of acquiring the needed skills and knowledge were extremely unlikely. The public universities are free as well but because of the fierce competition, it is difficult to gain admission. It is that competition that makes some of the public universities excellent schools.

During my time in Turkey, compulsory education was until the 5th grade. That same year it was raised to the 8th grade. Currently, the government is considering making it the 11th grade, the highest grade level in secondary education.

In addition to the higher quality of our school, we also learned the value of its location. On Friday night the week after our Istanbul excursion, Linda took us to Bilkent University Preparatory School or BUPS, another private school where her friend Jennie was teaching. We took a long taxi ride out from the city. The land stretched desolate and nearly treeless until we arrived at what looked like a small collection of cheap apartment buildings. A guardhouse allowed us to pass and we parked behind one of the concrete buildings and found Jennie at the top of the stairs.

"*Hoş geldiniz!*" she cried, It is nice you came!

"*Hoş bulduk!*" we responded, We found it nice!

She welcomed us in, showed us her impromptu bar, and introduced us to the guests. I sat next to a woman with a scarf, not on her head, but tied around her neck like a fashion statement. I wonder now if that was her intention or if she had to put it back on when she returned home. Her name was Birsen and she was a graduate student studying Ottoman history. She wore a bookworm's glasses and had a long angular nose and a round face of a light brown color. Her hair was long and black, and she frequently used a finger and a flick of her head to put it behind her shoulder.

I asked her about her classes. Birsen was learning Ottoman.

"I don't understand. They didn't speak Turkish?"

She explained that it was referred to not as Türkçe but as Osmanlıca. The Ottoman Empire was quite vast at its height, and much as anyone in the U.S. might use the word "tortilla" without thinking of it as Spanish, many words from Arabic, Persian, French and even Japanese were taken up by the Ottoman society. Atatürk's language revolution changed that significantly enough that one needed to learn the former tongue as a separate language.

When she found out I was from Madison, she became excited. "I want to study there!"

"In Madison? Why?"

I was surprised to find that at the time one of the best Ottoman history professors taught there.

"But first I must finish here. And I have a trouble with my professor. In fact, I don't think he wants me to leave. He can make problems for me." She believed it was because she was a woman. She asked me about Madison, the climate, the people. I had plenty of nice things to say, but when I mentioned bicycling she perked up. "Oh, I think if I ever go there I will do that. Here if a woman rides a bicycle, they look at you like it is bad." The truth was I hadn't seen many people at all on bicycles; it would seem to me a risk of life and limb with traffic as it was. We exchanged numbers and I told her that as soon as we had another party at the apartment, I would be sure to invite her.

Ankara would probably not make a list of must-sees in Turkey, but I found a lot of enjoyment in being immersed in it as we were. Though BUPS offered a bus service for students and teachers alike, to live on that compound would feel very isolated and the long ride into town would require serious consideration in any sort of plan to go out. I was very happy to be living in the midst of the local culture; I wanted to be one of them as much as I could.

Totally Turkish

I am not a shopper and feel like a whining five-year-old when I have to try on clothes, but the approaching winter demanded it. I stopped at Lights Market and asked Erdal if he knew a good place to buy a shirt. In fact, his cousin had a store, and Erdal came around the counter and began closing down the shop to take me there personally. He would hail a taxi. "No, no! Thank you very much! Um... no time. Other day." He shrugged, smiled pleasantly. I didn't want someone to close his store on my account. Networking, especially within the family, is a major aspect of business. *Everyone* has an uncle with a carpet store and a cousin with a good hotel. I walked a couple blocks, caught a *dolmuş* and headed for Ulus.

For weeks the sky had dripped gray, soaking body and soul, and I stepped from the *dolmuş* into drizzle. I found it best to romanticize it all, imagine an exciting movie set in a foreign country. The stores—nothing more than tiny garages with steel doors drawn up to reveal their wares—followed a meandering path up the hills of Ulus. The runoff rushed toward me and I stepped across on a few visible stones or pieces of cardboard dissolving to the consistency of the surrounding mud. Shopkeepers stood idly in doorways, occasionally hitching their pants and shouting to no one in particular, "Pants! Socks! Cheap, cheap!"

Overhangs of corrugated tin, canvas or plastic reached across the walkway. The crowd avoided the middle of the path where a long line of raindrops created a border between shop displays. A boy wearing a peacock blue servant shirt hustled past me toting a silver tray of empty tea glasses. Moments later he rushed in the other direction with full glasses haphazardly arranged but reliably balanced on his tray. Large burlap sacks of spices and dried fruits and lentils sat just beyond the reach of the falling sky. Fresh vegetables were the only bright colors and a table covered with bite-size fish shone like a collection of silver shards in the feeble light. The smell was there long before I saw it and well after I passed.

Not far from where the *dolmuş* had left me off I found a clothing store. An old man and his son helped me as I searched through piles of sweaters for something that looked Turkish. They held up various designs all made with wool, they assured me. Finally one struck my fancy, a light green sweater with a deep V neck that buttoned down the front. They convinced me to buy a black, long-sleeve, button-down shirt to wear underneath. I tried them on and they guided me to the mirror. I was wearing jeans and my black dress shoes. "Ah, there you are! You look Turkish!" the old man cried. I chuckled at the remark, but it was true. With my mouth shut, I wouldn't turn any heads in the market.

For my return home I sat at the front of the *dolmuş* and consequently became responsible for passing everyone's fare to the driver, who looked away from the road to sort through the tray of bills and coins to make change. "*Bir tane. İki tane.*" One person. Two persons. He passed back change and I handed it over my head blindly. Like fans buying hot dogs from their seats at a ballpark there is a system that transcends dishonesty and distrust.

When I returned to the apartment I flew into the living room spinning like a model, "Voila!" Chad and Bob looked up from the television and burst out laughing. "Totally Turkish!" I'd be wearing the sweater to work on casual Wednesdays. I wondered if anyone would notice if I combed up my eyebrows.

Temptation and Revelation

For some, a neighborhood pub might be considered one of life's staples. Feray, a fellow English instructor, told us her husband had a bar that we should visit sometime. Located on the ground floor of a high-rise in Kızılay, Temptation Bar had a front window obscured but for an upper right corner that looked like wrapping paper on a gift being peeled away for a peek.

The first night I went with Chad and Bob, the doormen stood like bank guards and told us we needed a reservation. We stood outside stumped. Another man stepped outside and lit up a cigarette. As I spoke to Chad about an alternative plan, I could see the man was listening. At the mention of Feray he interjected, "You are from Büyük Kolej?" Open sesame.

He was Feridun, Feray's husband. He gestured to the doormen, who immediately took our coats, and then he escorted us into a dark and crowded room. At the bar he spoke quickly to a tall man in a leather jacket who glanced at us and then stood up, offering his seat. The place was dark except for the bar itself, which curved into the room like a grand piano. Feridun bought us a couple beers and the bartender set a bowl of mixed nuts in front of us. Feridun made small talk before returning to mingling with the clientele like a mafioso casino owner.

The black walls were decorated with silhouettes of beautiful women painted in neon-colored paints that glowed eerily in the light from a small stage situated before a wooden dance floor. The band was fantastic. Many of the other bars in Ankara commonly featured a mediocre singer with a programmed keyboard that played canned pop songs to which the singer merely sang along. Glorified karaoke, I thought. But this was Hale and Her Arkestra: a bass player, a keyboardist, a drummer, and Hale, a nicely shaped nightclub diva with a powerful voice for both Turkish and Western pop. Her blue contacts glowed in the black light. On her break we struck up a conversation. She had grown up next to an American military base and her English was excellent; as a bass player for many years I am no stranger to late-night smoky clubs and we became instant friends.

Two nights later I was back with a beer and a bowl of nuts, learning Turkish pop songs. My bartender was İsa—Jesus in Turkish—and he made jokes of producing miraculous beers for me and getting someone served so he wouldn't be crucified. He spoke broken English and I had my smatterings of Turkish. He taught me more between serving beers, and as I was the only American in the place, I had plenty of opportunity to practice.

In the middle of Hale's show, the lights on the dance floor came up. Into the center danced a full-bodied woman—somewhat overweight by the anorexic American model standards—who wore an elaborate bikini decorated with sequins and dangling strands of fabric and tiny gold-colored medallions: a belly dancer. Her hair was bleached blond, something that Turkish men find appealing for its rarity and exoticness (thus the popularity of prostitutes from Georgia commonly known as Natashas). The dancing was provocative, the gyrating hips, the trembling belly, and the shaking of breasts. She went from table to table and the men hooted. As she leaned backward over each table, she twirled her hands around each other and the men either slid money into various parts of her clothing or stuck bills to her forehead.

During her set break Hale came over, kissed me on both cheeks and then introduced me to the man two barstools away, her fiancé, Tanzer, a clean-cut young bank executive from Istanbul. We toasted and drank. When Hale returned to her performance, we spoke of her. He was concerned for her safety knowing he was five hours away and she was at Temptation every night singing. At first I thought this was just some of the common Turkish male possessiveness, but there was a story. Hale lived alone, something unusual for a single woman in Turkey. Six months before, a man with a knife had broken into her apartment and attacked her. Her hands had been cut up but she managed to keep the attacker at bay and her screaming was enough to scare him off. The man was never caught, and Tanzer immediately found her a new apartment. She was still terrified and had asked another woman to move in with her. Every time Hale came home she went through all the rooms carefully turning on all the lights, sometimes with a knife in her hand.

After her final set I asked her about it. Hale told this story so nonchalantly that I almost did not believe her. She seemed indifferent and even joked about it. But a close look at her hands was evidence enough. Coincidentally, her new apartment was only two blocks from my own and on the way to school. I would be sure not to drop in unannounced.

The weekend after Halloween Chad and Bob decided to visit Cappadocia, a region of otherworldly rock formations. But Ankara was feeling like home to me and the recent excursions made me opt for a relaxing weekend.

Instead I received my first real beating from *rakı* at Temptation. Linda and Hasan had agreed to come out with me to my new hangout. Hasan never let me pay for anything and that night he financed my collapse. I was ordering rum and Cokes—*not* a typical drink in Turkey. Hale sat with us

during her set breaks and I was doing my best to make everyone laugh. And they did laugh. The next day I realized they
were mostly laughing *at* me as I was quickly becoming drunk
and had suddenly switched to *rakı*. Linda warned me: "Don't
mix *rakı* with other stuff. You'll be sorry." The music during
the breaks was loud and we were practically yelling over the
table. Hale had to speak close to my ear for me to hear her
and as she was also drinking, occasionally her lips brushed my
ear. The warm breath of a beautiful woman thrilled me and I
drank more. I was the center of attention. The crisp service of
Turkish waiters made me feel like the Sultan and it all kept
coming without me even lifting a finger. I even took one of
Hasan's cigarettes, though I don't smoke, and burlesqued
smokers.

We toasted: *şerefe!* This is the equivalent of "to your
health" but friends gave me varying translations. My favorite
was "Anything I say tonight please don't hold against me
tomorrow." Probably not the definition in the dictionary, but
I liked the idea.

Several drinks later, it was clear that I needed to be taken
home. Hasan guided me to the door as I sang the phonetic
near-equivalents of some of the Turkish songs. He and Linda
put me in a taxi and we rode to my apartment. "Are you sure
you're OK?" Linda asked. *Taaaaah-beeeee, eeeff-en-deeem*, I
slurred the response of cab drivers when they answered our
calls from the apartment, "Of course, my sir." Hasan helped
me out onto the pavement and opened the gate, which I
could not negotiate. I waved to them and turned to the door
fumbling with my keys for a *very* long time. I stood there
mumbling and humming and rattling when all of a sudden
Hasan appeared again and opened the lock for me. I turned
and the taxi was still parked where I had exited it. I waved
again and he caught the door before it closed on me and gently nudged me forward.

I came home to an empty apartment at three in the morning. Three, I thought. I attempted some math and perked up. So it's 11 a.m. back in the States! (Actually it was 7 p.m. the day before.) I got out my address book and began calling friends in the United States. I only managed to reach my friend Kris and she was baffled by my nonsensical train of thought and slurred speech. I tried to explain *rakı* to her but I think she had already gotten the picture. I hung up and grimaced at breaking Bob's commandment: Never drink and dial.

A cold sweat broke out over my brow and I rushed to the small bathroom as it was closest. As I lay down flat in a drunken stupor next to the porcelain hole in the floor, I thought how interesting it was that "worshipping the porcelain god" in a Muslim country matched their praying style just as it matched the Christian style back home. I also swore never to mix *rakı* and rum again.

A Hero's Day

Europe often looks down its western nose at Turkey, but what many fail to remember is that Turkey has been a democracy longer than Spain, Greece, Italy, Germany and several others. The national obsession with Atatürk, the man who brought this about, is a central thread in any story of Turkey. His many efforts at reform truly marked the republic from the rest of the Middle East. Its membership in NATO and its consideration for the European Union should be evidence enough. Change, however, no matter how beneficial, is rarely met without resistance and one doesn't need to search too hard to find evidence of a dictatorial nature to Atatürk's presidency; like a Franklin Roosevelt perhaps. "Government for the people, despite the people," he once said. So many years later, his fans still celebrate his life. I noticed that the Mooder, and some old men in the street, sometimes had their eyebrows combed up in apparent emulation of the national hero.

In 1938, Mustafa Kemal Atatürk passed away in his bed in the Dolmabahçe Palace in Istanbul, in a small room that lacked the opulence of the rest of the palace. The clock in that room remains frozen at 9:05 a.m., his time of death. Every November 10th at 9:05 across the country, time also stops. Everyone wears photocopied pictures of Atatürk pinned to their lapels and takes a moment to remember his life. I wore a pin that the school had given me. Everyone gathered in the auditorium and after a loud siren, stood for a moment of silence. The morning classes were cancelled for a trip to his mausoleum there in Ankara.

I boarded one of the school buses in front of the school and one of my prep students joined me. Out of the corner of my eye I could see her staring up at me.

"How are you teacher?"

"I'm fine thanks, and you?"

"Very well, tanks. You have go to Anıtkabir... before?"

"No, I—" I stared at her in disbelief. Had she just used "have"?

She continued. "I have been there... um... three time."

My face would have been the same had my camera bag asked me to lift it to see out the window. "What is your name again? Meh... Mer..."

"Merve, teacher."

"Your English is very good." Prep students were still struggling with present tense and even more basic things; this attempt before me was incredible.

"I love English class, teacher. You are my favorite teacher. I like to practice my English." She had never opened her mouth in class, yet here she was talking my arm off as I sat with my jaw in my lap.

She was my assistant that day, proudly carrying my camera bag. The kids were well behaved, due in part to the presence of the sterner Turkish teachers. The mausoleum, at the end of a tree-lined walk past crouching lion statues, was a columned building like a smaller Parthenon. The design sought to incorporate elements from all the different civilizations that had occupied the land throughout history. Each group of students took turns paying respects. Then we entered a nearby museum filled with memorabilia of the founder of the republic.

Interred nearby was a man whose name I hadn't heard before, but upon hearing his story, his historical importance was clear. Ismet Inönü, like Atatürk, had led successful campaigns against the Greeks during the war for independence after the defeat of the Ottoman Empire in World War I. He became the first prime minister in 1923 and served alongside Atatürk. He became president after Atatürk's death and, most importantly, kept Turkey neutral for the Second World War. He remained in politics up until his death in 1973. I learned later that he was Kurdish in ethnicity.

In keeping with the nationalist feelings of the day, we toured a military facility north of the city. We weren't allowed to take photographs, and foreboding signs along the fences outside emphasized that fact. It amounted to a tank show. Standing behind a plexiglass shelter we looked on as a soldier in a tank used a powerful mounted machine gun to take out cardboard targets that flipped up before him on a shooting range. The students oohed and aahed as if we were watching fireworks. Down the road we watched from a set of bleachers as a tank ran through ponds and over short concrete walls, showing its maneuverability.

We ended our tour in a courtyard near the main gate where the various tanks of history were on display with placards before them. The teenage boys gawked at them with fascination. One of them turned to me proudly, "Teacher, Turkey is very powerful. You see? If someone attack us, we destroy them. We fight anyone."

In a moment's annoyance with his nationalism and youthful idealism of war I was tempted to point out the placards that showed all the tanks were American. The Turks had an important ally behind them.

But that fearlessness has deep roots; Turks have a long history of warriors. They descended on Anatolia on horseback from Asia, precursors and cousins to Genghis Khan and his fearsome entourage. They had given the Crusaders hell, surprising those knights in heavy metal armor by running circles around them firing arrows with deadly accuracy. They had a reputation for tenacity and sometimes brutality in the First World War—the Australians respectfully dubbed them Johnny Turk when they miraculously held Gallipoli against the Allies. A friend in Wisconsin had served alongside Turks in Korea and said they were tough as nails and hunkered down without complaint in the harshest of conditions. I could see that nationalism, so strong among even my youngest students, would fan the flames of war very quickly if history ever went that route again. Frankly, it scared me.

Fortunately, the Turks were spending more time practicing the fine art of bureaucracy. Back at school Linda had some bad news for us. "You will need to leave the country and go to the nearest Turkish embassy for your work visas."

The three of us stood stunned.

"Now don't panic, this is our fault. The school will have to pay to fly you to Cyprus."

"Cyprus?"

"It's the closest option and the easiest."

"Sounds painless," I said.

"Sounds better than painless," said Bob.

Linda shrugged. "It's the rule that you have to get the work visa *outside* the country, but we've always done it this way. This is the first time they called us on it. Oh well."

We weren't about to protest.

Cyprus

Cyprus. An island, a stepping stone across the Mediterranean Sea. A theatre for so much history. Occupied, stolen, reoccupied, finally divided. A possession of the Roman Empire, of Alexander the Great. Christian, Muslim, pagan. Temporary home to King Richard the Lionhearted when he marched beneath the Cross to face Saladin in the Holy Land. A prize of the Ottomans, the Venetians, the Lusignans, sacked by the Egyptians, and laden with artifacts dating back to the Neolithic period. Now divided between the Greek and Turkish Cypriots, embittered against itself, but maintaining a tentative peace as two protégés of bigger rivals. But that November weekend it meant the closest Turkish embassy.

Cyprus is two countries. In 1974 when fighting between the two ethnicities finally went full scale, the Turks moved north, the Greeks south. Each side blames the other and its corresponding mother country. Lifelong neighbors were suddenly citizens of disparate nations. The rest of the world—Turkey excepted—refused to recognize Northern Cyprus.

The one-hour flight took us in over a range of mountains, the Five Fingers, and let us out onto the tarmac in a balmy 75 degrees. We were given tourist cards but customs did not stamp our passports. Greece or Greek Cyprus would deny entry to anyone bearing a stamp from the unrecognized Turkish Cyprus. The customs official also gave us each a pamphlet listing the alleged atrocities that the Greek Cypriots had committed against Turkish Cypriots.

There were five of us including Jim and Joan, and we took a taxi from the airport to Lefkosha where we needed to find the embassy and our hotel. As we peeled out into the left lane on the highway, my heart leapt into my throat for a second as oncoming traffic blurred by us on the right. Traffic drives on the left in Cyprus, its inheritance as a former British colony. We exercised our Turkish with the driver, and Chad hit him with his old standby: "*Futbol?* Beşiktaş? Galatasaray? Do you like?" I always wondered if we received an accurate fare when Chad came out and said Beşiktaş was his favorite and the driver turned out to be a Galatasaray man.

We checked in and immediately set out exploring our surroundings. Our first site in Lefkosha was Selimiye Mosque, originally a cathedral to the Lusignan kings in the thirteenth century. From our balcony we could see it clearly, three blocks away. It was not quite 4:30 on a Saturday and already the streets were empty and nearly all the shops were closed. As I approached the mosque I came upon a man, shoes off, bent solemnly in prayer just outside the front door. The doors looked boarded up and I wasn't sure if one could enter, though the tourist information seemed to indicate that it was still an operating mosque and the primary one in Lefkosha. Ornate stone carvings and gargoyle-like figures jutted out over me along the edge of the roof. Just as at Ayasofya in Istanbul, there was a mingling of two religions in stone. Selimiye seemed dressed more like its original role of cathedral, but one could see the wires up into the steeples where the speakers and the voice of the muezzin had supplanted bells. The adjoining building, some kind of meeting hall, bore the figures of saints carved in relief. In the fading light I snapped a photo of Jesus on a table sitting up and surrounded by apostles.

We continued wandering, finding blind alleys and curving, narrow streets. Our eight-story hotel was the tallest building in sight. The rest were squat, concrete boxes, unappealing to the eye but for the red-tiled rooftops. Before the final light faded from the sky, we found a street closed to traffic and lined with plastic tables. When we turned the corner, several waiters looked up from their bored stupor with interest. The owner of the closest restaurant was the quickest to act and we were hustled to a table.

We weren't very hungry so we only ordered tea. He said, "*Çay yok.*" There is no tea. We hesitated and he rattled off a list of foods that we had no interest in. But there is no such thing as "*Çay yok*" in Turkey (or Turkish Cyprus). When it looked like we might move on, he remembered there were some tea bags somewhere. He sent out a waiter. His name was Cuma, which is Turkish for Friday. Our man Friday, an excitable young man, was eager to use his English. We answered questions for him about ourselves. He thought we were with the UN. A modest peacekeeping force defends the border between the two Cypruses which runs along the outskirts of the city. Around the corner a block away from us stood the neutral ground, a stretch of abandoned buildings and empty streets enclosed in barbed wire.

Cuma said work was scarce in Lefkosha and he dreamed of moving to Germany, a very popular Turkish ambition. Over 1.8 million Turks live in Germany already. He had learned all of his English from waiting on tables. He offered to pay for our tea but we refused. Sometimes the kindness was masochistic. We thanked him and promised to return on Monday.

From there the streets became very dark. Auto and artisan shops took over. Cats skirted our footsteps; an occasional stray dog, pathetic and unthreatening, hesitated in our path and then loped past in a wide arc. It was reminiscent of old Ankara or the poor districts of a Mexican city, as though poverty and the hard life always dressed the same. Venus was bright in the sky but the moon still hadn't appeared. We passed through a small unlit park where the skeletons of swings and monkey bars lurked around us, and as we spoke, someone took notice. A whispered chattering in Turkish and then a bold "Allo?"

We stopped and peered into the dark along a chain-link fence. "Hello," we answered.

"Hello" was the limit of the speaker's English and the rest of the conversation took place in Tarzan Turkish. Two boys scurried up to us eagerly to investigate the foreigners who perhaps had lost their way. Even in the feeble efforts of a streetlight halfway down the block I could see how stiff their clothing was from dirt. Their hands were clutched into pockets of pants that hung loosely as though their balled up fists were the only things holding them up. Their faces were covered with smudges, and their hair looked less like something human and more like the tangle of straw and pine needles that robins thread their nests out of. Before they arrived, their stench did. They introduced themselves and I cringed as I shook each hand. When I pulled mine away, it too took on the smell of human excrement that hung around us now.

With a mixture of revulsion, pity, and outrage at their extreme poverty, we let them lead us to a wooden door to what appeared to be a museum. They insisted on knocking, though clearly it was after hours. The door creaked open like the castle of the villain in a movie and the yellow light spilled out like a false heat and revealed the stones we were standing on. An old man stood in the doorway puzzled, and the boys asked if we could see the museum. He told us to come back the next day and we smiled dumbly and pardoned our way off his front step. He smiled then, bewildered at the mixed company that had disturbed his quiet evening.

As we walked, one of the boys stopped and opened an abandoned car that rested on its rims, and crawled inside giggling. The gutted car, the ruins of the modern century, seemed just another feature of the playground. They walked with us as far as their home before bidding us goodnight. We stared into the lot with wonder. Piles of garbage, glass, and scrap metal lay everywhere within the fenced area. Paths wove in and out of them. The moon, now rising, cast a silvery gloom over it all like the color of dirty bones, and with closer scrutiny we were able to make out what looked like half of a large metal holding container. It stood like part of the rest of the garden of refuse, but an orderly stack of plastic crates on either side of the pathway made it clear that it was their home. Junkyard kids.

We knew we needed to rise early the next day and so we bid them goodnight. Back at the hotel we settled in on our sixth-floor balcony and watched the pigeons settle in to their own roosts along the ornate stonework around the roof and windows three floors below us across the street.

We talked about the fear of heights and how simply throwing something off the balcony (like a bottle cap perhaps, to see if we could wake the pigeons) could give each of us a lurching sense of falling. When I was a child I used to get the same sinking feeling in my stomach when I let a helium balloon slip away into the sky. I'd feel like falling down and clinging to the grass, as though I might fall off the earth as well. Looking down at the pigeons and imagining the arc of a bottle cap touched on the memory of that emotion.

There is a tendency in some of us to project ourselves, as though the forward motion of one's arm could drag the body along with it, as if some sense of self could drift off into oblivion with a pink balloon in a cloudless sky. Perhaps that same tendency—the tendency to fully experience and understand our surroundings—forces those of us who are fearful, but conscious of it, to follow someone else through a few steps of life. Perhaps it is what forces me to try to imagine the desperate and undignified steps of a small boy, unaware of the thoughtlessly wasted riches and the unshared plenty that lay beyond his rusted, chain-link fence. The stones of the city's wall protected him from the perversions of the West but showed no pity for his poverty. However, I couldn't share his numbing unawareness, just as I couldn't know the dulled pangs of hunger that had gone on so long that they had worn down their teeth. I put my students in his shoes and it frightened me to see what we would inflict upon an innocent child. How many resources and lives had the Turks and Greeks wasted in segregating Cypriots by ethnicity? How much work was the UN putting into maintaining a line in the sand? What was the benefit for this boy?

It's good to be fearful, to the extent that it doesn't paralyze you, but rather forces you to confront what you'd prefer to turn away from. The sight, the smell of a human child left like refuse in the street leaves the fortunate thankful, the compassionate indignant, and the selfish unmoved. It is a moment of real education that everyone should be required to witness as long as such poverty exists in the world.

Too Interesting

The living proximity and the abundance of our time together eventually trespassed a bit on personal space. I found myself sometimes breaking in on Chad's leisurely pace, like an excitable puppy begging to be taken for a walk. Chad was a poet and not typically an early riser. I had learned that he needed his quiet moments on the balcony or in a cafe with a book or a notepad. Bob became more and more enthusiastic about the Turkish choir he was singing in, which gave us all a little more room to breathe. Nevertheless, we often moved in a pack.

Even an unusual environment soon becomes the norm and a routine evolves; we developed patterns. Buy a Coke for the walk home. A liter of sour cherry juice and a kilo of olives. Eat *pide* at the same restaurant. Stop each day to talk to Hasan the Police Officer and ask him the same list of small talk questions about the weather and the weekend. And we started to say *We*.

"How was Cyprus?" asked Linda back at the English office.

"We thought it was very interesting," said Bob. "We really liked the castle there and we enjoyed the food a lot. There was a great seafood restaurant...."

Chad interrupted. "Bob, you have to stop saying We. I feel like we are one person all of a sudden. Don't always speak for the three of us. That's becoming a bad habit."

I shifted from foot to foot knowing that I had been doing

it a lot as well. It was true the abundance of our time together created the strange I/we dichotomy where opinions and perspectives shifted back and forth between personal and communal, not always with accurate results. *We* lived together, *we* worked together, *we* often ate together, and *we* traveled together. Now we were speaking collectively.

Bob apologized and I thought the reprimand may have stung. Chad perhaps thought the same and admitted that he did it as well but that *we* needed to avoid that. "And stop saying 'interesting.' What is interesting? What does it mean? What makes something interesting?"

Here was Bob's strength: he found that amusing, admitting his tendency to vaguely sum up an experience as simply interesting. He laughed at himself and it became a sort of house joke. "Hey Bob, how's that chicken kebap?" "Interesting!" he'd reply.

Later in the day I stood in the hall watching the chaos, munching on a coconut candy bar from the *kantin*. Students ran, shouted, played tag, hung out the windows even though the air was starting to get brisk. And in the midst of all this, I heard a bellowing voice. From the chaos rose a tiny island of order: Jim. Our time together on the Cyprus trip and a few classroom suggestions that had worked brilliantly had planted a seed of admiration in me. He stood amidst the river of children, directing them to walk not run, and in an orderly keep-to-the-right fashion. It looked exhausting and the results were unclear. Surely when he left, any progress would be swept away. But I had to admire the guy for trying.

Chad came up to me with a cup of coffee, briefly observing Jim's plight. "You won't believe what Sarp said today."

Sarp was a chubby little genius from one of Chad's sixth-grade classes. On casual Wednesdays when he didn't have the benefit of the uniform, he dressed nerdishly and his careful diction reinforced that impression. But his penchant for performance endeared him to classmates. He frequently moon-walked like Michael Jackson and had the dance moves and lyrics down from Will Smith's "Men in Black." He watched a lot of television in English and it had clear positive effects on his English.

"He said, 'Gravity is exceptionally strong today, teacher. I noticed many students' pencil boxes falling off their desks.'" Star Trek was one of his favorite shows.

That night we had to meet with parents to give the first grades. Prior to the event we had had to make the grade books. We were given strips of tiny ID photos for all our classes. On the floor in the living room we sat with scissors and rubber cement, placing each photo with the corresponding student. That was the easy part.

When we returned to school that night we sat in student desks awaiting parents. There was a translator for every two teachers in each room. I prepared some key phrases and left Linda to handle Jim's translation until I got stuck. "Good student. Participates in class. Should raise hand more" (this one done in pantomime).

All was going well and I was just starting to get comfortable when the mother of Candan, my eighth-grade challenge, sat down in front of me. I stammered a bit but then said what had to be said. "Her behavior is bad. She talks in class. I had to send her out once." Her face was difficult to read but the next day I had a new friend in class so I assumed my point had been made.

One last mother sat down across from me. To my relief she spoke English. "My daughter, she loves you too much." I blushed madly. "Er... I..." My mind raced, but they told us nothing about what to do or say in a situation like this in teaching school. But the mother was smiling. I relaxed and chuckled a bit. Many of the Turkish students had quickly learned a casual use of the word "love" and often substituted "too" for "very," changing the flavor of a statement. "I love pizza too much" sounded like a problem when it merely meant the speaker meant *very* much. I thanked her and told her she was too kind.

Christmas in Turkey

Turkey may be a Muslim country and not very close to the North Pole, but Christmas turned out to be more than I expected. Saint Nicholas lived and died in Turkey. In Turkish he is known as Noel Baba (Father Christmas). He was a Christian bishop in the fourth century in the town of Demre. Legend has it he dropped bags of coins down the chimneys of the houses of the unwed village girls who had no money for dowries. With this money the young women were able to marry. He is the patron saint of virgins, not surprisingly. Raiders from Italy stole his remains in 1087 but some allegedly survive in the Antalya Museum on the Mediterranean.

My uncle once worked several years in Saudi Arabia where he wasn't even allowed to receive a Christmas card from home. But even though it wasn't a Muslim holiday, the Turks were open to others celebrating it. What I didn't expect was the overwhelming spirit and love that I felt for not just one day, but an entire week of celebration. Parties were plentiful. Dilek had us over to her apartment for an English department dinner. Shala took us along to an international party with ambassadors and other embassy workers. We were invited to a Turkish-Filipino Association Party (who knew?) and another at the Filipino embassy. Our Iranian friend Nader's wife Dolores was from the Philippines. Nader was an electrical engineer and had had "troubles" with the Iranian government. Now he had his own business in Ankara. He didn't like Turkey much but appreciated his freedom. I asked him if he was Muslim. He smiled, raised his hands and whiskey, and proclaimed, "Oh no, I am free." In her eight years in Iran, Dolores had been taken to the police twice: once because it was hot and she had let some of her hair slip out of her veil and a second time because she was pregnant and during her last trimester the increased girth raised her dress just enough to reveal part of her ankle. Another woman had dragged her downtown. The two gave us a clearer picture of how secular Turkey compared to some of the other Muslim countries of the Middle East. They became part of our "family" for the holidays much like Linda and İffet.

Christmas arrived suddenly, without the long buildup from November. The commercial aspect, however, still existed. Kızılay turned up a notch. Where it had been crowded before, it became nearly frantic. People were waiting outside Dost bookstore just for the crowds to thin out inside. The streets became full of *satıcı*s (street vendors) selling every imaginable item. Several shabbily dressed university students stood blowing into their hands and selling pirated CDs. When a police officer meandered through the scene, they were quickly stacked and placed into a duffel bag until the officer passed. Trinket salesmen peddled key chains, necklaces, earrings, and candles. A couple vendors displayed pictures of Atatürk, or music legends like Jimi Hendrix or Jim Morrison. Almost as popular as Atatürk were the Che Guevara photos. I also noticed many copies of Che biographies at the booksellers that spread their wares out on tarps. Greeting cards—some in English, but also Turkish Christmas cards—lined the sidewalks in wire stands. And I could always find a man roasting chestnuts on an open fire. He used olive oil cans crafted into a grill and roasting pan. The chestnuts were doled out in cups fashioned from old newspaper pages and the aroma wafted among the trees and milling shoppers.

Returning from shopping, we stopped to chat with Hasan

the Police Officer. He told me the latest *futbol* scores and commented on the weather. His casual posture took some of the edge off his authority; memories of him kicking a ball back and forth with some boys with his gun in hand made me think maybe we had a slacker on the beat.

But as we struggled to create small talk beyond the weather, a passing teenager collapsed in the street and he ran to investigate. He whirled to return for his gun and snapped it up like a soldier who had been suddenly called into a firefight. The boy sprawled across the pavement, trembling with a seizure. Passersby stopped with concern and the call went out for an onion. One magically appeared quickly enough to draw attention, as though one were always kept on hand for emergencies. A woman administered an onion half like smelling salts and eventually the boy found his bearings.

Hasan returned to his post, pointing to the boy as he disappeared around the corner. "A trick." Hasan had seen him before and claimed it was some kind of beggar's scam. He offered me a cigarette like he always did though I repeatedly told him I didn't smoke.

Hasan lived on the other side of the city, not far from Ulus. His rent was much less than ours but I knew that didn't mean it was cheap. I had seen other apartments when I had helped a friend search for one. Often they were unheated and renters owned small electric heaters. Some were single rooms with bad light, and bathrooms that consisted of the porcelain-framed hole in the floor, a small sink, and a sloping floor and drain under a shower nozzle that looked more suitable for watering plants. The circle I was running with had middle-class incomes or better; Hasan didn't have the benefit of sharing a flat with family, and his girlfriend was not likely to move in without being married. He asked about our apartment and I told him the school provided it. He only nodded as though he had suspected as much.

For the first time in my life, I *cringed* when I woke on Christmas Morning. For weeks I had felt that perhaps teaching was going to break my back and the days were ironically getting longer in December. I couldn't maintain classes and felt I was teaching little if anything. But I had my best Christmas gift waiting for me in the classroom.

We started talking about holiday memories but of course they didn't have any Christmas ones. So they explained Ramazan (Turkish pronunciation of Ramadan) a bit to me. Thirty days of fasting and it follows the Muslim calendar, shifting every year. That year it started New Year's Eve.

"Teacher, where you will go for semester holiday?" "Well, I was thinking of Iran." "TEACHER! NO! Teacher, why?" They implored me like children whose father just said he was going to end it all. We went on about the misconceptions everyone has about the other half. I was surprised by how they generalized and I taught them the words "prejudice" and "stereotype." It was easy to get them to see because I came from a place that in many cases thought the same of Turkey as the Turks did of Iran. Many people called Turkey a third world country, backward, dangerous and Muslim (another stereotype: that these words are synonymous) and thought that they rode camels, wore turbans and lived in a desert. "Really?" Yes, really. "But we don't, *hocam*." Of course you don't, but they don't know that. "Tell them." I do, of course. But think about it. Where do they get their information? How do you know Iran is dangerous? "Because on TV they..." Exactly. The media.

A little history lesson, I told them. I told them what I knew of the 1979 Iranian Revolution and the Hostage Crisis and how the media commanded the 1980 American election. And how that image of Iran has stuck in the American mentality with little further input for twenty years other than an illegal arms sale to Iran under the Reagan administration, which apparently had been quickly forgotten. In the fourth period we discussed the difference in ethnicity in Turkey and how those people were portrayed on television. The Kurdish situation brought that theme to the forefront. At the time, the Kurds were banned from using their language on television and, by the average non-Kurdish Turk, were considered suspicious. This was probably entirely creditable to the media's coverage of the Kurdish rebels in the East. But I heard the same thing several times from my students: "This is Turkey, teacher. If you live here, you are not Kurdish or Armenian. You are Turkish."

"Can't one be both? Who was here before the Turks?" I asked.

They knew this of course. It is their history. Many foreigners believe the Turks and the Arabs are the same people, but that couldn't be further from the truth. The Seljuk Turks came down from Asia during the 11th century. "Teacher, you know this?"

"Of course, I read about it. In fact..." And I told them what I knew of the historical conflict between Islam and Christianity and how it became so deeply rooted during the Crusades. And there it was before me. A class of students not talking, only listening, their eyes watching me. Laughing when I told them of a castle defended solely by sheep that a group of Crusaders passing through Syria, overwhelmed by hunger and religious fervor, had laid siege to. Raising eyebrows in amazement when I told them Christians had raped, pillaged, and plundered fellow Christians in Constantinople during the Fourth Crusade. They were asking questions, and answering and discussing the ones I offered. I felt the satisfaction, the momentum one gets when doing a job and doing it well.

After a good day of teaching, we went home and wrapped our gifts. Linda lived only two blocks from us so we were the first in the door. As the other guests arrived—Ayşe, İffet, Joan, and Jane—we greeted them at the door. We embraced İffet warmly, kissing her on both cheeks and saying Merry Christmas, Mom. The group consisted of the foreign English department plus Ayşe, the assistant principal for the middle grades. Linda had prepared an Arabic dish for us: upside-down rice with chicken. Her apartment was new and she only had a love seat in her living room, so we arranged ourselves on the floor in a semicircle. When Chad opened his gift—the soundtrack to the movie *Hamam*—we all fell over with laughter.

A *hamam* is a Turkish bath where one goes for a long process of steaming and rinsing that ends in a brutal massage more akin to Greco-Roman wrestling and a scrubbing that damn near takes your skin off and makes you wonder why the devil you shower every day if all that dirt and dead skin still remain. A barber up in Ulus had recommended his neighborhood *hamam* as a very old and traditional one. Bob and I had been dragging our feet about going and finally Chad had ventured off on his own. When I had arrived home late from school that day, I found Chad with a dazed look on his face, seated in front of the television but not really watching. "How was it?"

He thought a moment, "Um... not so good. I think Tuesdays might be gay night at the *hamam*." Perhaps smelling new blood and seeing Chad didn't speak the language, a couple strangers had propositioned him using graphic hand gestures. Chad clucked his rejection hastily with raised eyebrows and lifted chin - tsk, tsk, tsk! - but tried to remain calm and go about his business. But soon after, he walked into a curtained room to rinse some more and found two men engaged in sex. He changed directions and tried to calmly pack up to leave. Chad said he was only a little shaken, because he never felt he was actually in danger, just horribly uncomfortable. It was only finally when someone grabbed his butt, that he fled into the street. We weren't sure whether to laugh or do the Turkish wag of the head and "tsk, tsk, tsk" but Chad's storytelling decided that for us. Any mention of the word "*hamam*" was a guaranteed belly-laugh.

It conveniently rhymes with the Turkish word for "OK" - "*tamam*." So invariably someone purposely slips and substitutes them. "Want to go to a movie?" "*Hamam*... er, sorry, *tamam*." The whole English department heard the story on several occasions and every time we started the story, "Chad went to the *hamam* in Ulus..." we got raised eyebrows and half smiles. Everyone knew you don't go to THAT *hamam*. As wonderful as this place could be at times, we couldn't forget it was real and not without its seedier elements. Where our naiveté could give us a deeper almost childlike curiosity and fascination about the world, it could also lead us blindly into situations that could have been avoided. When İffet stood up to take a picture of us at the Christmas party, she said, "OK everyone, say '*hamam*.'"

Disillusionment

The Saturday afternoon before Christmas, when we were returning from the market, a family had been moving into the basement apartment. We called the Ask Linda line and with a little investigation she found out the *kapıcı* had been fired. Strange, we thought, but his wife Elif came that following week to clean anyway.

The same night someone knocked on our door. I opened it to find our neighbor from across the hall, a tall mustachioed man with a dull look to his face but the swagger of someone who had money. We typically only exchanged simple greetings in passing. His posture made it clear he had to tell us something. I wondered if our occasional house soccer matches with a taped up ball of socks in the hallway had finally been too much.

He spoke very minimal English. "The cleaning woman... um... finish."

"*Efendim?*"

"No woman here... She no come... building."

"She is our cleaning woman."

He frowned, struggling to be clearer. We understood the message but that was not enough.

"Yes. But no more... Other woman. This one, no."

"She works for us. Our apartment."

He became agitated. "No... she no come here."

We stood at a bewildering impasse, and he left.

The next day I was called from my class to the office. I

knew it had to be something extremely important to interrupt me. I entered the English office and all hell was breaking loose. Chad was already there. Our neighbor was there. A flurry of Turkish told me it was not a friendly visit. He didn't look at us, but only spoke to İffet. Our neighbor was the son of the building owner. We could no longer employ Elif. We argued that rent was paid and it was no business of his who we hired. He disagreed. The argument went back and forth and İffet spoke softly to me. "You are right, of course. But the school works with these apartments." So he was threatening. I made my stand. "Fine. I can move out." The man was beet red and spittle flew from his lips. I couldn't imagine what could elicit such a reaction. Later Linda told us that Elif had somehow insulted the man or his father. But then she added that probably Elif had rejected an advance. That was speculation of course. I can remember Elif and this man's wife frequently chatting in the hall; they appeared to be good friends. Was this all just a matter of male ego?

The door to the office swung wide and the Sultan himself stood there in a furor that trumped anyone else's in the room. "Why are you not in your classes?" We scattered like mice, fearing Müdür's wrath. Linda told us later that he had given our neighbor an earful for interrupting class; we were exonerated. We didn't need Elif's services again until after the two-week semester break a few weeks later, and when we asked Linda to call her for us, she told us she had lost the number. I suspected she had done that on purpose but only to prevent me from hanging myself. It wasn't my battleground, but convictions pay little heed to maps and border crossings.

The treatment of women in Turkey is a mixed bag. Certainly the conservative Muslim men of the countryside are accompanied by veiled spouses who often walk a pace behind them. But even in those settings, the woman does demand a certain respect within the hierarchy of the home. Atatürk at one time had banned the veil and fez, and though veils are legal once again and have returned among some of the religious, they are not worn with the frequency one associates with Arab countries, and almost never cover the face. University students were prohibited from wearing them for ID photos and at times this was a point of contention.

If a man stopped to ask directions when I was walking with a Turkish woman, all eyes would turn to me automatically, despite the fact that I made all physical gestures of deference. He would seem baffled when I allowed the woman to handle the whole thing.

On the other hand, there is an impressive presence of women in the professional work force. Engineering programs are no longer strictly male departments and Turkey has already had a woman prime minister, something that many countries, including my own, have failed to produce.

In the evening on Friday, the day after Christmas, and two weeks before our confrontation with our brutish neighbor, the faculty and some important parents were gathering in the snack cafeteria and around the adjoining swimming pool. When we returned to the school, the doors were locked and the lights were out. Only the lower-level door in back was open. Music rose up the spiral staircase that leads down to the pool and the *kantin*. My glasses fogged over when we walked into the humid air and it took me a few minutes to orient myself. I found Ayşe and Ebru Dark standing next to a table of snacks. I grabbed a *rakı* from the bar and made toward them to hang out with them for a while. I admired Ayşe for her independence, her commanding presence. When I sent students out, they paled visibly if they were destined for her office. She was tall for a Turkish woman, blond, heavily built. Despite an attractive face and a quick and warm smile, something in her unwavering gaze said she was not to be messed with.

Ebru Dark was a strikingly beautiful woman with olive skin, black eyes, gleaming white teeth and long black hair just past her shoulders. She was in her early thirties but she could have believably claimed 24. We joked around some, and then, as is so natural in Turkey, the lights went out. Everything was suddenly quiet; the band, of course, ceased and its last strains echoed back from across the pool. When the power came back on about a minute later everyone resumed as if nothing out of the ordinary had happened. As I looked around the room it just seemed like everyone had frozen and patiently waited to be reanimated by the light. I laughed shortly and Ebru looked at me with the bemused smile of one who wonders what they missed.

I asked her if she was going to Ebru Blond's wedding that night; we were all invited. She said no. I asked why. "Because Ebru had to limit the number of guests. Spouses aren't supposed to come and so my husband can't go." So come with us. "My husband won't let me go alone." I dropped the subject like a dead rat. We faltered a bit before picking up on another topic. This wasn't unfamiliar to me. Her mother-in-law lives with her and they hate each other. She missed every one of our parties and I could tell something was amiss when she finally told us defensively that Turks simply don't have parties. I felt terrible and wanted to say something, but it was clearly not my business.

Rumi and the Müdür started the champagne bottles popping and as the corks bobbed in the pool I wondered if any faculty would be doing the same by the end of the night. Already there were Turkish dance lines hand in hand kicking their way around the edge of the water. The Müdür, red-faced and no doubt carrying some *rakı*, was leading a pack of them himself. For such a stern figure he always became a lively sultan when the kids weren't around. I was roped into a circle for a few jigs and slipped away when I could. I found İffet, Ferit, and Dilek at a plastic deck table across the pool and sat with them to observe the festivities. The band started playing one of my favorite Turkish pop songs and Dilek insisted I dance. "Do you know how to rock 'n' roll?" What I thought was a line from a bad movie script was Turkish for swing or jitterbug. We twisted and spun along the lip of the pool and I nearly jitterbugged her into the drink, which she teasingly insisted was my plan all along. And maybe it was. We made plans to taxi over to Dilek's and ride with her and Ersin to the wedding. (Apparently *some* spouses were allowed.)

The wedding was held on the outskirts of Ankara at a military complex. We were checked at a guard post and directed to a lone hotel-looking building in the center of a dark and seemingly empty field. In the lobby we found what I liked to call "flowers on a stick," large wreath-like floral arrangements on the end of a staff of wood resembling a giant lollipop of blossoms. They were present at all celebrations. When we arrived Ebru Blond was signing some documents with her new husband as the crowd looked on from their tables. And that was that. No ceremony, no special dances, garters, or thrown bouquets. The modern ceremony of the city. Occasionally I'd pass women in the street with their palms dyed dark with henna, part of a more traditional matrimony.

For the dinner I sat with İffet and Dilek. The Müdür and his wife Güneş sat opposite me so I tried to behave a bit. We toasted several times and I felt that tenderness of mutual admiration between me and my adopted family. But I felt guilty, as though I were hiding something. I hadn't told İffet that I would not be there next year, but surely Linda had. It felt like a betrayal.

İffet tested my Turkish and as usual held me out to be better than I really was. The Müdür nodded sagely and toasted again. He said something gruffly, and İffet translated and asked for her own curiosity: "Why are you trying so hard to

learn Turkish if you are never going to use it again?" I
shrugged. "Because I love to learn. I am not happy if I am not
learning something. That's part of the reason I went into
teaching in the first place. Always something to learn. At my
previous jobs I merely found the repetition of mundane tasks.
I hated it. Even learning Turkish gives me a sense of progress,
of development."

İffet patted my hand. Another toast. We watched each
other for a few seconds. She knew. Turning to Ferit, I broke
the silence: "So when are we going fishing? I am not leaving
until I catch a fish in Turkey." İffet smiled. I knew from the
start I would love İffet. I knew our relationship was one of
many she would have and had had over the years with the
American teachers, but I believed this one was one she would
cherish like few others. I still believe so. She was "Mom" after
all.

The waiter came around the table to take our orders for
coffee, carefully noting how each person wanted it. I ordered
mine *orta*, medium sweet. İffet stifled a laugh and spoke aside,
"It doesn't matter. He will bring *all* of us *orta*." Since the
sugar is added to the pot as the coffee cooks, varying the
sweetness means multiple batches of coffee.

Afterward we shivered a bit in the night air as we took our
turns with lengthy goodbyes which were standard for us now.
Everyone was kissed, everyone hugged. It was a moment of
such unabashed fondness, one of those times when I really felt
I was faced with something real in my life. The bonds of
blood are strong but the ties of acquired loves are special in
that there is no reason for them other than one's choosing.

Ramazan Stakeout

I crouched down in front of the radiator along the wall and shadowed from the meager light from the front window. Through the semi-transparent curtains I watched the empty street below, a child hiding in a dark corner, hoping to catch a glimpse of Santa Claus. It was the fourth night that I had risen at three a.m. to keep my shivering vigil. It's the drums. They woke me and I lay there matching their beating with the frantic beating of my heart. My head was always full of the fragments of a broken dream and I was dizzy and disoriented. It took me several moments to untangle myself from my covers and identify what was growing in a steady crescendo outside my window. I'd run down the dark corridor, sometimes with a blanket wrapped around me, but every night the street was empty and the echoes dissipated even as I watched. One night the swirling of sound among the concrete buildings rose and fell so often that I ran to the window three times only to be disappointed.

It was Ramazan, the season to be hungry. Drummers pass through the city streets somewhere around three a.m. to awaken the faithful for breakfast. Every night they invaded my dreams, leaving me shaken but determined to see the elusive drummer marching up and down the hills.

Just before sunrise, when the first call to prayer drifts ethereal over the rooftops, the fasting begins. From dawn until dusk nothing must pass the lips; no food, no drink, no cigarettes, no toothpaste. One is not even allowed to lick a stamp.

Following the Muslim calendar, the dates of the thirty-day holy month changed each year. That year it began December 31. When I arrived home from school that first day I was ravenous, waiting by the window, listening for the call to prayer signifying the suspension of the fast at sunset. At school, as word got out that we were *oruç* (in the state of fasting), we started receiving mixed reactions. Students, amazed, first asked, "Teacher... Muslim?" I explained to them that we were doing it to experience more fully what it was to be in Turkey, maybe to understand the concept of fasting as well—and on a personal level just to see if I could do it. The other teachers looked at us with curiosity—some of them kept the fast, others ignored it completely. In our department, a couple simply thought we were crazy. İffet told everyone, partly in admiration of our attempts to be part of the culture and partly in amusement. Dilek seemed almost bitter about it. She told us we were stupid. I speculated on this for some time, thinking, What difference did it make to her? It occurred to me that I had treated Bob the same way when he had talked about searching for a Protestant church in Ankara. I had given up regular mass attendance back in college and come to terms with what my religion meant to me and the character of my spirituality. The things I rejected perhaps threaten me in a way; possibly they represent the guilt that comes from breaking rules that—though I no longer abide by them—are as much a part of me as my appendix. Unlike functionless organs, however, these things are not as easily parted with.

Dilek was part of a wave of liberal change in Turkey during the seventies. With the current political situation being a battle between secularism and religious conservatism, any hard-liner progressives were going to reject the dogma associated with the "old-fashioned" way of doing things. Dilek's mild disdain made more sense to me.

Though I didn't feel any purer or closer to the higher

power by fasting, I must admit I gained some insights. I like food. A lot. In fact, when deprived of it, food is just about all I can think about (which is exactly what the pure faster is to avoid doing). I also realize that I snack unnecessarily throughout the day. If there is anything edible lying around, I will put it in my mouth absentmindedly. Several mornings I caught myself picking up a handful of pistachios and spitting them into the sink as though I had just mouthed poison. I wasn't even hungry yet. At around 4:45 (and about two minutes later each day) I stood at the refrigerator waiting with my bag of olives and a loaf of special Ramazan bread listening intently for the call to prayer. Then the feasting would begin without any regard for recipes or appropriate combinations. Dip a loaf in yogurt, eat a tomato like an apple—it didn't matter. And oh, the flavors!

At school I found my energy draining from me. By the afternoon it seemed like I barely had the strength to raise my voice. The handful of fasting kids and I scowled at each other until the final bell. But they were very supportive. "How many days teacher?" Ten. "Oooooh teacher, wery good!" Driving became just that much more dangerous. Taxi and *dolmuş* drivers were not about to be cut off. They drove around blind with annoyance, the radio on, waiting for that call from the mosque to come over the airwaves. Bob and Chad once stopped while in a cab so that they could go to the trunk and remove candy bars from their bags. The driver took the opportunity to attack a bread loaf which he drew from under his seat.

Bread was suddenly hard to come by. Like Eastern Europe in its hard times, people stood in block-long lines outside the bakeries waiting for the big bang. The end of the fast is often marked by the firing of a cannon.

But the only pounding noises I heard were those in my head. By the thirteenth day I was coming home and raiding

169

the aspirin bottle before the bread box. I was definitely losing weight - something I really didn't think was healthy considering my meager build. And on the sixteenth day, I fell from grace. It was the day we were told by the administration that all our students might be taken from us for the second semester and we'd have to start from scratch with a new bunch of 235. I thought of all the time I had put into developing relationships and searching for discipline angles. I immediately stalked to the cafeteria and bought a handful of coconut candy bars and devoured them in anger. The fast was over. Dilek smiled when she saw me. "Sixteen days!? Well, don't worry. You are a better Muslim than I."

A Picnic with the Hittites

Just like with tax systems, religions often have their loop-holes. It was the weekend after New Year's Day and we were several days into the fast trying not to be grumpy. When I was in Catholic grade school, we couldn't eat meat on Fridays during Lent. Hardly as challenging as not eating at all, but nevertheless a religious demand that was to be met. At school it meant processed fish patties on a regular basis. At home, however, my mother believed my brother and I were "grow-ing boys" and should be spared any sort of alimentary chal-lenge that could affect our health. (A meat and potatoes cul-ture looks warily on anything resembling vegetarianism.)

My mother and Allah must have had some kind of con-nection. One of the allowances for the fast is that pregnant women, the infirm, and certain travelers can be exempt. Travelers? We rented a car for Saturday.

Our destination was Hattuşaş, the ancient capital of the Hittite Empire. "Hittite" was a word that sounded vaguely familiar. Much like Ephesus and Antioch, names slip off pages of old Bible lessons and onto the road map. In Turkey histo-ry lies atop history like the fine layers of a good baklava. The Hittites date back to around 1900 BC, invaders like so many civilizations to follow, but of uncertain origins. They captured Hattuşaş in Central Anatolia and set up their capital there around 1800 BC, eventually extending their reign from the Black Sea down into Syria.

This was our first driving experience in Turkey. From the daily exposure to automotive chaos, we were all a little apprehensive. Chad took the wheel and Bircan and Bob the back seat. We stopped for olives, bread, and dried apricots, and then we were on our way out of the city, heading to the mountains.

We watched trucks pass on blind curves as we wound our way higher into the Anatolian plateau. It took a few hours but we found the turnoff and rolled into the quiet village of Boğazköy. We parked in front of the local museum and took a break to stroll past a collection of local archaeology that the Anatolian Civilizations Museum (and various others in the world, no doubt) had passed over. It isn't often that one can step outside a museum onto the soil the artifacts had been dug up from.

Just outside town the road curled up to the site. We parked the car and walked out onto a wide hill, nearly treeless, covered with a pattern of bricks and stones that resembled a labyrinth. In most places Hattuşaş doesn't even come up to the knee, but for me it was one of the most magical places we visited.

There is a sense of place there. The sun pierced a clear blue sky and I looked out over the village below. The red-tiled rooftops sat among fields plotted out for agriculture, the tin roof of a small mosque gleamed under a heatless sun, and smoke from heating or cooking fires drifted up lazily from simple lives. As we were at a higher altitude than Ankara and it was January after all, the temperature was brisk; I wore a winter jacket and kept my hands in gloves the whole time.

We were reading the blueprint in stone of the capital of an empire. Temples and great palaces, common houses and stables are now rendered equally as mere foundations. I passed over thresholds trying to imagine the invisible doors and walls. We strolled down a main street of cobblestones and a Turkish boy pointed out a few details I might not have noticed. I would not have recognized the temple. On the floor of the entrance he showed us the deep grooves of what must have been a very heavy stone door; caught like a photograph of motion, a blurred scratch represented years, maybe centuries of comings and goings.

I tried to imagine crowds of Hittites going about their business just as the Turks were doing in the valley before me. The names change, the empires topple, but villagers still live and breathe, their buildings decay and crumble until the next generation fills in the holes and mends the rafters, or simply moves down the road to start over again.

The surrounding mountain peaks were bright with snow and curved around the plateau like larger fortifications than the man-made ones that were part of the magnificence of the city. The cold peaks heightened the sense of isolation. What I called isolation, a Hittite strategist might have called protection.

History is a lonely place. The voices are gone, the language itself reduced to the surviving fragments of ancient scratchings in stone. And the written tablets have been carried off, scattered by the curiosity of men to distant glass cases where any unwary museum patron might overlook the invisible hands and now silent tongues that inspired them. There are no Hittite recipes or dances or music though there surely must have been. The rooftops and even the walls have been laid low and but a footprint remains of the city. But the sweeping wind and the remaining stones that resist it have a gravity that captured my imagination.

A young boy in the parking lot came up to perhaps the only tourists he might see all day—or all week even—and tried to sell us various handcrafts fashioned into the surviving images of Hittite gods. I bought a flat black stone scratched white in the shape of a two-headed eagle and hung on a nylon necklace. Another god rising up from the earth to be carried into another life.

The fortifications of Hattuşaş once ran along the edge of

the city. Much of them remains, a massive wall of stone along a ridge that drops away to forest on the side opposite the village. We drove the car up to a gate in the wall that featured a giant stone lion on either side, an impressive way to greet guests at the door. We climbed along the wall like children atop a fallen beast, and we separated to pursue our own imaginations. I stared down at the forest below, imagining invaders eyeing the defenses, a steep climb that could not be taken at a run, and then the mammoth wall at the top.

In the middle of it all was a tunnel, formed with a corbelled arch, which ran from behind the fortifications down to the small meadow between the slope and the forest. Ice was frozen into cracks and crevices, and as I entered from below, I felt along its uneven surface. As with many ancient constructions of large proportions, I am forced to marvel at the ingenuity of a machine-less work force. The tunnel gave the Hittites a way to send out troops to flank encroaching enemies. The frozen mud beneath my feet had been formed and unformed by marching soldiers at one time.

I closed my eyes and I could hear the voices. A couple of children. Passing out to the meadow to collect some flowers. Chatting and teasing in a language so unintelligible to me, but made familiar by laughter. Just regular people, not some exotic grandiose name of king and conqueror, empire and army. Hittite children on a Saturday afternoon. They came closer, playing games in the darkness of the tunnel, their voices twirling down the jagged rocks. As they came nearer, words emerged from the bubbling vowels and consonants, Turkish words. I opened my eyes and a mother and her two young children appeared at the mouth of the passage. They were surprised to find me there, motionless and silent, but then greeted me with smiles. They continued their frolicking in voices subdued by the presence of an oddly silent stranger, and disappeared up into Hattuşaş.

Winter in Istanbul

We took our winter holiday in Egypt and so spent a couple days in Old Istanbul where we found a hostel across the street from Ayasofya. Though it was January, bright green grass grew up along the brick patterns of the streets and in the cracks along the stone walls. Istanbul was cold and damp, and the wind whipped in off the Bosphorus. We spent a day wandering the streets of Taksim on the European side of Istanbul, wearing several sweaters and stocking caps, ducking into tea shops whenever the cold became unbearable. In Ankara it was snowing.

We hung about Sultanahmet Mosque that first night, snapping pictures and staring at its reflection in the still fountain water out front, like a misplaced constellation made up of the Ramazan lights strung around the minarets. Street vendors sold us *sahlep*—a thick drink traditionally made from hot milk and the powdered tubers of orchids and served with a sprinkling of cinnamon—and *boza,* a sort of nonalcoholic fermented bulgur drink—thick, cold and tangy with a light carbonation. The spotlights on the giant mosque and its six towering minarets made it look like a magical castle fit for fairy tales.

The markets were crowded with the approaching end of Ramazan. We bounced between vendors like ping-pong balls. My breath swirled on the air, unsure of where to go. People did the same, jostling me a bit as they passed in search of Ramazan gifts. The following day would be the first day of three of Şeker Bayramı, the holiday that ends the fast. Traditionally everyone buys chocolates and other sweets for the house for guests who might come to call. Also, much like Easter for Christians, it is common to buy new clothes for the event.

We stepped inside the halls of the Grand Bazaar, covered high above with inverted brick cups like a giant brick muffin pan supported by stone columns—the Ottoman style. Common wares were grouped together. In one room of the halls one can find nothing but jewelry; in another, only children's clothing or colorfully decorated porcelain plates or just socks. Traditional Ottoman outfits, bright red, green, or blue satin lined with glittering gold lace and buttons, hung side by side with Chicago Bulls sweatshirts and baseball caps. A man stopped us outside his porcelain shop and gave us a demonstration reminiscent of infomercials. To show the quality of the porcelain's glazing, he poured lemon cologne on it and lit it with a Zippo. The air blurred above it with alcohol flames. I chuckled and the vendor took this as encouragement to light the plate a second time.

We returned to the open air and the damp, aching chill that saps the will more than straightforward bitter cold does. I stood in the middle of the street "listening to Istanbul with my eyes closed," like the famous Turkish poem by Orhan Veli. One can feel something powerful there. Maybe it is the history built atop history or the cramped feeling of a city of over twelve million. Or the proximity of one cold sea flowing into another just beyond the marketplace. The bright songs of songbirds in cages somewhere challenged the oppressive weather and made me appreciate how the world resists the simplistic dichotomy of beautiful or ugly days. We had wandered the streets all the way to the waterfront where the wind off the waves seemed to penetrate with an ache like a cold bruise and I hardly noticed the grandeur across the bridge and

Galata Kulesi, a Genoese-built tower that rose up as a counterpoint to the palace and mosques of our side. The smell of
fresh fish lingered in the dampness and several carts were covered with anchovies, lifeless and dull under the clouded sky.

We awoke to cannon shots from the mosque signifying the
end of Ramazan and set out to the Asian side to meet İffet at
her mother's apartment for dinner. After a delightful meal we
sat in the living room for Turkish coffee. Our drinks came out
strong and gritty and in small shot-sized cups. Just about
every Turk can spend a good ten minutes telling fortunes
from the silt at the bottom of the cup.

After drinking it we covered the cups with our saucers and
flipped them over. We waited for the grounds to cool before
looking into the cups to find our fortunes. İffet did all of ours.
If the cup dripped, it meant tears. In Bob's case, they were
tears of happiness, according to İffet. A woman was in his
future. Mine revealed five long journeys, a tall, thin woman,
an elephant, and no tears. I'll be damned if I knew whether
that was good news or not.

Hanging on the wall was a round blue glass about the size
of my hand with a dark circle within a light blue circle within
a white circle. I had seen so many of them before in varying
sizes. They were common in shops and markets either for sale
or hanging as decoration. Taxi drivers had small ones dangling from their rearview mirrors or key chains.

"İffet, what *is* that?"

She smiled, "That is *nazar boncuğu*; it protects you from
the evil eye."

I raised my eyebrows. "Does it work?" I winked at the
superstition.

It was designed to reflect it. "People do not completely
believe it, but just hope that it might protect them. But most
people including me believe that jealous eyes always bring bad

luck, and people have lots of stories that could prove this belief. I mean it doesn't belong to only the urban culture. Some people do other things to get rid of the evil eye. Some melt lead and pour it into cold water over the head of a person in order to break an evil spell, some break something made of glass, and some carry an amulet called *'muska'* with a prayer written by a *hoca*."

The evil eye is not just Turkish. Much of Mediterranean culture harbors a belief in the curse of a bad look. It dates as far back as the Bible and has origins in Egypt where the eye was considered so powerful.

İffet's eyes lit up. "Two years ago we planned to spend a weekend with all my cousins. We were twelve people. Add the husbands and wives and the children, we became thirty-six. We decided to go to a hotel in Kızılcahamam. Some of us went there from Ankara, some from Istanbul, some from Samsun, and my sister from Amsterdam. One of my aunts called each of us before going and asked us to break glass when we arrived there, thinking that everybody would be jealous of us and something bad would happen. We all promised. The first day we became a little drunk, we broke three bottles of wine—of course after we drank the wine—and kept our promise." Her cheeks glowed with the memory.

Amoebas for Souvenirs

Days after our return from Egypt, I found myself sitting down halfway through lessons and teaching from my desk with a cold sweat. My only relief was the fact that at least my students hadn't been switched to Chad's class as had been the administration's plan before our vacation. Enough phone calls from angry parents or perhaps just one important one, had convinced Rumi Bey that Müdür's plan was not good for business.

But my sense of victory was short-lived when my insides turned on me. I gave the students things to do so that I could simply observe and concentrate on surviving the day. I ate a lot of yogurt as was suggested by many Turks for stomach troubles and I kept taking over-the-counter medicines. But when it became clear that I was bleeding internally, I could no longer count on wishful thinking. Terror of terrors: I had to go to the school doctor. He spoke no English, but occasionally broke into German—of which I knew nothing. So I grimaced as I looked up Turkish words I never thought I'd need to use, certainly not in mixed company. We squinted at each other over a medical encyclopedia and Turkish-English dictionary like a stare down over a chessboard. What I hoped for was a broad smile and a reach into the drawer for some antibiotics and a good chuckle. What he gave me was an address. It looked like I was going to be spending some time as a lab rat.

The school provided some health coverage as part of my contract. It covered the school doctor and the same socialized coverage that all Turks receive at public hospitals. But the system is overwhelmed and underfunded, which means crowded waiting rooms and less than first-rate service. Private care is costly for Turks but recommended in many cases. I went the private route with the lab work and for me it was affordable and efficient.

My results came back and the school doctor sighed over the fax I gave him. "Ah." His bushy, gray eyebrows sloped beneath thick lenses that magnified his pores. We struggled through the anatomical vocabulary and I glanced meekly at the nurse until we arrived at the verdict. "Amoebas." Amoebas? "Amoebic dysentery." As of that moment my insides had a lot in common with a country pond. I shrugged, relieved to have an answer, and watched as he filled out a prescription. One of the janitors would deliver the meds to me in my classroom. When the package arrived, there were only twenty pills and I had seven days to take them. This seemed like a quick and easy fix. How wrong I was.

I awoke the next morning suffocating. I tried to sit up, but couldn't. What was pinning me to the bed was my blanket. The world, my body included, had turned to lead overnight. Chad popped his head into the room, took one look, and told me not to worry, he'd cover for me. Taking a day off was not easy, as it didn't mean the school called a sub; it meant your teaching partner took your entire load into his own classroom with his own class. I grimaced with guilt, but realized I had little choice.

My body adjusted to the medication enough so that the next day I was able to make it to school. I spent a lot of time leaning heavily on my desk. On the way home I smacked my tongue and asked Chad, "Is it me or is the pollution really bad today?" He shrugged, "No worse than usual." The air tasted like an aluminum gum wrapper. When I arrived back at the apartment I called İffet and read the label off the medicine. In addition to the lethargy and the foul taste, my stomach was turning, my head was pounding and dizziness plagued me whenever I stood up. The tablets were designed to create a hostile environment within my body and it became clear that they were succeeding.

I counted the days and the hours to my last pill. With the debilitating effects of the medicine, I hadn't noticed when the symptoms of my actual illness disappeared. As near as I could tell, I was cured but I still needed to return to the lab to repeat the tests. My enormous relief dwindled when the school doctor told me I needed to test again in a month to be sure that eggs didn't remain. Eggs? I grit my teeth, hoping there was a misunderstanding. I called İffet for translation. The bottom line was this: if anything made it through the treatment, it could mean serious problems later on—"serious" meaning liver infection.

The illness and the week of side effects had beaten the spirit out of me. Winter still dragged on. Anxiety over my next year's employment didn't help. I had already decided not to return to Büyük Kolej, but to acquire another overseas job would be difficult. The job fairs were in distant countries and taking off enough time from work would be tricky.

As Linda and the Turkish teachers had predicted, the second semester moved quickly. Egypt was soon a month behind me and still I had no leads on work. Jim and Joan, however, returned from Izmir on the Aegean coast after a long weekend, with tales of wining and dining with the headmaster of another private school there. Their excitement was infectious. The Aegean Sea, a beautifully landscaped campus, and an administration that had an apparently stricter and more "American" discipline policy—all made this new school an attractive package. Within days I had e-mailed and set up an interview.

As days passed, my mood began to cloud over as much as

the Ankara skies were clearing up. A vague sense of loneliness compounded my frustration with the classroom. I came to doubt everything: Izmir, Turkey, even teaching itself. I finalized the time of the interview for Saturday and bought an overnight bus ticket. Friday night, Chad, Bob, and I sat at a nearby bar for an hour, keeping casual conversation and laughing like old men enjoying the same routine they had practiced for twenty years. The location didn't matter, this was a moment of being "home." Two friends and a few drinks put off the anxiety of a big decision that loomed beyond the peaks of Ankara.

My brothers patted me on the back as I left, gripped my arm in support, and wished me luck with the same confidence I had—that I was a shoe-in. Outside a taxi slowed down and I gestured for it to stop, mumbled the bus company's name and address to the driver, and fell into a trance staring at the Galatasaray *futbol* emblem that dangled from the rearview mirror.

I awoke at the bus station, boarded my bus and started to chat with the old man sitting next to me. He was eighty-five, old enough to remember Atatürk. Just then the bus next to us started rolling forward, giving me the momentary illusion that ours was rolling backward, awakening a strange, uncertain feeling in me. When the tail of the bus passed my window, I saw one of the station attendants pass behind it, and as he did so, he swirled water in a cup in his hand, and with a flick of the wrist, scattered the contents across the back of the departing vehicle.

"What's that?" I asked the old man.

"Tradition. We do that also to the bride and groom when they leave. After the wedding. So they return soon and safely."

I leaned against the window and wondered.

The Last Supper and
My Descent into Hell

I wandered in and out of consciousness. Visions of a pure face leaning over me, a warm, bitter fluid passing over my tongue, words slurring into a monologue of mercy, understood only from the tone. As my eyes focused, I saw a white curtain ballooning in the breeze in the dim light. Outside the window the world crouched in the shadow of a canyon wall, and as the desert air crawled into the room, its heat dissipated on the marble floor. A woman, her face framed by white cloth, not a single hair escaping, leaned over me again and handed me a cracker. I remembered the crackers. I'd bought those. From outside the window came a distant brassy cry of a trumpet; drums rattled a cadence but not loud enough to disturb. It evoked a victorious army marching home.

The woman spoke but it wasn't Arabic. My mind tried to catch the words, pick them apart like an untrusting prisoner examining food slipped into his cell. French. She spoke French. It was Easter. The music. I heard singing, voices meek beneath the proud blasts of horns. The curtain swirled like a spirit into the room until the breeze slipped by and the transparent material alighted once more against the sill.

The woman helped me sit up enough so that I could sip at the teacup she held forth. I whispered *shokran,* thank you in Arabic, and she smiled. She left the room and I curled into a ball around a debilitating feeling of nausea that reminded me where I was. Ma'aloula. A small town in the Syrian desert. In a convent.

My interview in Izmir had landed me a job and a couple weeks later spring break arrived. That year it coincided with the Muslim holiday Kurban Bayramı, a celebration of Abraham's willingness to sacrifice his then only son, Isaac. At the last moment God stops his hand and instructs him to slaughter a ram in Isaac's stead. School was out for a week and many families purchased rams for slaughter for the occasion. I took this opportunity to visit nearby Syria with my friends Cedric, a French archaeology student, and Canan, a Turkish woman studying the same.

We had traveled by bus down through Antakya, biblical Antioch, where Arab and Turkish culture mix, and over the border into Syria. Holy Thursday found Canan, Cedric, and me wandering through the tangled streets of the Christian quarter in Damascus. All around us were Syrians who had taken to the streets to commemorate the Last Supper. Horns blew and children marched by, dressed in uniforms that looked like boy scouts and girl scouts. Drums pattered in alleyways, doorways glowed with lights, and worshippers spilled into the many churches, some of which were celebrating mass in Aramaic, Jesus' own language. A glass coffin, filled with floral arrangements, draped with a white cloth, passed us with a brass and drum band of middle-school children. As we entered the courtyard of one of the churches, two teenagers at the gate pasted religious stickers written in Arabic onto our chests.

Our guidebook led us to a basement chapel of coarsely constructed brick walls where St. Paul and some of the first Christians had secretly held worship. When our energy began to wane, we wandered down more secluded, narrower streets, sensing that our night's adventures were just about through.

We would soon need to head back north to Turkey. Passing a cookie shop, I noticed Santa Claus in the window. The owner understood some English and brought chairs out for us, sending word in to his family in the house next door to prepare tea. He brought out a cassette player and played American pop ballads from the 1980s: Lionel Richie, Chicago, and Barry Manilow. It was as I sat there, enjoying the slight chill of a clear-skied night with an unlikely familiar air, that I began my descent into hell.

The surface of my tongue grew taut with the bitterness of the tea and I felt my stomach following. By the time we said our thank-yous and rose to leave, I began feeling sharp stomach pains. I passed it off as a possible adverse effect of the caffeine and, back at the hotel, I curled into a tight ball and fell into a fitful slumber with the flimsy mattress cupping me like a hammock.

A couple hours later I awoke to stomach pains. I donned my shoes and flew from the room, down the hall to the bathrooms. From behind two battered wooden doors arose a horrible stench, and the sight of the floors banished any hope that they had been cleaned recently. I entered one with a toilet and bathtub, and went into a violent fit of vomiting into the tub. My head pounded with a rush of blood and I sat down weakly with a fit of diarrhea to match. Half-seated, I slumped over the edge of the tub, cold sweat on my brow. My vision became fuzzy and a tingling red closed around me until I could only see a small circle of the bottom of the tub. What I saw there seemed impossible. Food from two days previous, still partly digested. I fought to breathe against the beast in my throat. I wondered why I hadn't woken up my companions. Would they know to look for me? Would they find me in time? Where was a hospital? How would I ask for one?

I had never been that ill before and as I regained my breath a new fear crept into my mind: dehydration. I am not one who pays proper attention to drinking a lot of fluids on a hot day and I know that I don't consume anywhere near the recommended amount of water. I was losing everything I had at an alarming rate. After an hour, though the pain had not subsided, the nausea had diminished enough for me to sit up. With shaky hands I used a plastic pitcher from the corner to rinse out the tub. I fumbled with the door and guided myself with a hand on the wall back to our room. In the stale darkness I curled into a fetal position and faded away.

But I only stole a few moments before consciousness shattered open and I was running again to the bathroom. The second round was no less intense than the first. How much could I endure without medical intervention? I was too weak to feel horror, just a dull sense of doom. Half an hour later, I returned to my bed, shivering.

Morning came fast and the sun burned brightly around the edges of the thick shade but none of us stirred. I remembered with gratitude that my companions were late sleepers.

Just before noon they decided we had to leave. I told them I had been ill, but I don't think they understood and I didn't give any details. Cedric suggested we go to Ma'aloula, a desert town where Aramaic is still spoken. I grimaced at the thought of another bus ride but held my tongue. I sipped water, but wetting my lips instigated nausea. The sun was brutal and I struggled to keep up with Cedric and Canan. We walked several blocks and found our bus. "Tell the Partridge family someone stole their ride," I muttered. It was a rickety affair painted in a bizarre blend of neon colors.

A scattered crowd came together and we all filed onto the bus. I sat with my knees against the seat before me and clung to a window for air. I unfolded a plastic bag from my pack. Canan became concerned, beginning to realize how bad I was. The bus left the station rattling over uneven streets and

I spent most of the ride with my teeth clenched. I watched as our urban surroundings gave way to sun-bleached and rocky terrain. My stomach curled and lurched at every bump and I teetered on the edge. We stepped off the bus onto pavement that radiated a half day's worth of sun, and I stopped short as if my body refused another step. "Guys? I can't do this. You can go on ahead, but right now I just need a bed. You can get me when you're done."

Cedric and Canan helped me purchase crackers at a shop and then lead me along the sidewalk a few paces to a wide marble staircase up into a shaded courtyard. They left me on the steps and went inside on my behalf.

"We found you a bed. The nuns here have several rooms for travelers. You can rest here as long as you like. It costs nothing."

An Easter miracle. We followed a nun who spoke only Arabic and French and they left me in a clean room with two beds. A breeze drifted in through the window. I worked off my hiking boots and collected myself in a lump across the bed. I must have been sleeping before my friends had even reached the street. It was Good Friday.

A couple hours of rest proved to be insufficient and when Canan and Cedric returned, I made a serious decision.

"*What!?*"

"I mean it. Go ahead without me."

"Are you *sure?*"

"Positive. I insist. We can meet tomorrow at Homs."

Cedric and Canan hesitated, caught between their concern for my health and the revulsion that illness evokes. To be sure, they were reluctant, but I also knew I would feel more anxious and guilty if two people were waiting for me and sacrificing valuable vacation time. My only concerns were rest and fluids. I didn't need help with that. The logistics of getting to

Homs—a city halfway back to Turkey—mattered not at all. We decided on a place and time, and I sent them off with relief at not being a burden. I drifted back to sleep.

Until the light came on, that is. I didn't even lift my head; I merely angled my eyes down over my cheekbone. In the doorway stood a short man of about forty, with salt and pepper hair, Arab features, and a bushy moustache. He greeted me in Arabic.

Whatever tiny phrase I managed in reply, it had the effect of convincing him I knew Arabic. He began to question me. My brow furrowed in frustration. "I don't speak Arabic."

To accommodate for my obvious lack of comprehension, he began shouting and repeating himself. Not angrily but with the methodical patience of an experienced torturer who knows he will finally prevail and get an answer. He sat on the other bed and watched me and I rolled to face away from him. Whenever I was about to cross the border of dreamland, he called me back. I managed to make myself understood regarding my illness. Certainly that was more evident from my pale and feeble appearance than my poorly pronounced bit from a pocket phrase book. I also told him my destination was Homs.

His face lit up and his bushy eyebrows jumped into his forehead. His eyes were wide enough that I could see white all around the irises. We now had the name of a city as a common language. "Hooooms?" he bellowed, stretching out the vowel. He stuck his hand out, twisting it at the wrist as though jiggling a doorknob—an interrogative gesture in the Middle East. "Hooooms?"

"Yes. Homs."

He nodded.

The Easter music had ended to be replaced by this man's mantra—"Hooooms?" Whenever his fruitless questioning reached a long pause, he'd throw open his eyes, jiggle that

doorknob, and confirm my next day's destination—
"Hooooms?"

"*Yes! Homs!*" I thought I'd go mad.

He changed into flannel pajamas and alternated between pacing and sitting on the edge of the bed. There was a meek knock at the door and a young girl entered.

To my surprise she spoke up in uncertain English. I raised myself on an elbow and smiled. I asked her questions but her English was quite basic. They were from Lebanon and visiting for Easter, I discovered. The man cut in and attempted to explain something.

He pointed and said "baby." The girl is his baby? I thought. OK. Something about "boy." Something about "gone." Something about "bad," about "Lebanon," about... I was lost. Did this little girl *have* a baby? And a man who had left her? She looked twelve; his wife? I shook that thought away. The girl smiled uncertainly and eventually the man gave up. I lay back down but kept watching them. He stared at his feet and she crossed her arms. Moments went by and then the man's hand came up: "Hooooms?"

"*Yeees*, Homs!"

Satisfied with this answer, he nodded to the girl and repeated it, "Hooooms" and pointed at me. He sent the girl away and she said good night to me. He finally turned out the light, and I fell asleep.

By morning, my mind had grown sharper. I swallowed a cracker and another swig of water. The man was gone and I packed quickly. In the courtyard, the nuns hustled me into a dining room and insisted I eat something. They gave me bread and a sour-smelling cheese. I politely refused the cheese but nibbled some of the bread which was enough to stir my stomach. I thanked them and rose to leave just as my Lebanese friend entered. His eyes flew wide and his eyebrows flew up like a broken shade: "Hooooms?"

I left some money in a jar outside what appeared to be an office. The nun there smiled at me and nodded her gratitude. I expressed mine as well. But she held me by the sleeve a moment, calling to someone inside. A nun emerged with a message in English: "Your friends are in Homs?"

"Yes?"

"They call. You meet them at 4 o'clock. At the clock tower."

Why did they call to tell me something I already knew? Did the nun confuse the message? Outside the convent, a shopkeeper told me to take the bus to the highway. When the bus arrived, the man explained to the driver. The bus circled back toward the highway and when we arrived at the intersection there were two choices: right to Damascus and left to Homs, Aleppo, and, ultimately, Turkey. He stopped the bus and opened the door. "Get out." I stared at him in shock. He explained that another bus would pass. As the bus sped off toward Damascus, I crossed the hot asphalt to the dusty pull-off on the northbound side. I stood in the middle of a rocky, arid wasteland with a backpack, half a bottle of water, and the sun beating down on me. Not a soul in sight. I chuckled absurdly.

The rumble of a bus called me to action and I waved at it. It blew past me without even slowing. Another absurd little chuckle rose in my throat as I watched it disappear over the next rise. But the crunch of tires through crushed stones turned me around as a van pulled up. The driver—a stocky man, mid-thirties, mustachioed—leaned over and flipped open the passenger door. I appreciated the irony: "Hoooms?" I jiggled the invisible doorknob.

"Yes, Homs." Another miracle. Homs was a two-hour drive.

His name was Mohammed. He spoke English rather well. As with many strangers I had met on this journey, he was surprised and perhaps impressed that I was an American traveling in Syria. Without exception, I had been met with kindness and curiosity at every turn. The conversation with Mohammed followed no particular course but he did find an opportunity to point out how good it was to have two wives. Later we came to the subject of cola. Syria was the only place I had ever visited where Coca-Cola and Pepsi hadn't invaded. He wrinkled his nose. "Coca-Cola is bad. It has cocaine in it. It has caffeine too. We don't allow this. In Syria there is RC and Double Cola." This surely was not Turkey.

I arrived in Homs with time to spare. Three hours in fact. I turned my attention to finding a place to rest. The manager at the first hotel I entered would not rent me a bed for only a couple hours; the man at the second hotel agreed after some hesitation and a bit of haggling over the price. Then he looked at me shrewdly and asked: "Are you American?"

"Er, yes I am."

"And you are traveling with a Frenchman and a Turkish girl?"

The hairs on my neck rose. "...Yes."

"OK."

"OK." I paid him up front and he led me to my room. The sun reflected off the concrete walls outside and the room filled with a soft glow. I collapsed on the rough fabric of the spread and fell fast asleep with my hand covering my eyes.

I found Cedric and Canan at the clock tower and I told them I'd be continuing on to Turkey that night. They helped me find the correct minivan back to Aleppo. From there Turkey was a short ride over the border.

I told them about the strange question at the hotel and the message at the convent. They too had been received with recognition at that very hotel the day before. From what we could piece together, the nuns must have called ahead to look for the two of them to make sure I wasn't being abandoned.

Then upon hearing that the nuns had called, Canan and Cedric called the convent to reconfirm our rendezvous. Not as unsettling as it first seemed.

They waited at the station until my ride rolled into traffic, and I braced myself for another two-hour voyage. We only stopped once, when the van hit a biker with the passenger mirror and everyone got out to pass the bike and rider around, shouting and inspecting for damage. Then we continued on.

"Turkey tonight? OK." The man ran his finger down a paper before him on the counter. "I will check. Please..." He indicated for me to sit, stepped outside, and returned moments later. "I am sorry. Bus is not going tonight. Next bus tomorrow in morning. You need place for stay? This is no problem. I have hotel. Very cheap, very clean." He was drawing me a map when a man came and told him something. He smiled. "Now there is bus." For the first time in a couple days I felt hopeful.

My bus was a double-decker and I took a seat on the right side, three rows back from the driver's seat. The cushioned seats absorbed all sound like I was sitting in cotton and I realized I was alone. The air was stale and held a strange chemical odor. The carpeting along the floor was dark with stains and grime, but at that point I didn't care. Fifteen minutes later, three men stepped on and one started the engine. I drifted off to sleep.

I awoke to the silence of the seat cushions again; the engine wasn't running. Outside the window I saw gas pumps. I frowned, Couldn't they have filled up *before* such a small trip? A row of blue plastic barrels stood alongside the pumps and I saw our driver rolling one, along the edge of its bottom, past my window. When I heard a grunt and heavy footfalls up the stairs and across the second-level floor above me I realized these barrels were the passengers that were so conspicuously lacking. I whirled about, stunned. What was in the barrels?

When the last barrel was loaded, some of the attendants began dragging barrels out of the station as a fat, unshaven man at the pump waited to fill them with... *diesel fuel?* I stared with dull amazement as he stood with one hand holding the nozzle and the other a *cigarette*. The men wrestled each one onto the bus as it was capped. They began hoisting them onto the seats across from me. All the while, I was invisible.

The three men climbed aboard and we were on our way. The fumes were stifling. I'm riding a giant, double-decker bomb, I thought. There were at least fifty barrels. And now I was an accomplice. At the border the Syrians stamped my passport without question. I got off the bus at the Turkish side, glancing about, waiting for God knows what to happen. The customs official greeted the drivers with recognition. The driver shook hands over the counter while handing the man a five-million lira note. I looked away and kept my eyes to my own business, but they certainly didn't appear to be hiding anything. The official spoke to me in English and I tried to answer everything in Turkish. I am a teacher. In Ankara. From America. On vacation. He stamped my book and we were gone. At the gate where vehicles are typically pulled aside and searched, one of the bus men gave a package of tea to the guard. We were over the border in less time than I've ever taken at any other border in my life.

Moments later I stood in the crisp night air of Antakya. Though my head still ached, my limbs were still cramped, and my insides still churned, I was home. I was safe. I could falter a bit with the language but be understood. I staggered along the street until I found a hotel. The clerk eyed me warily, but found me a room. I took the elevator to my room, threw my things on the floor, flung off my clothes, and crawled under the covers.

Someone knocked. I whimpered in frustration, but

climbed back out of bed and into my pants. I opened the door without caution, and standing there with a polite smile was a man with *postcards!* At *one in the morning?!* I stared at the cards as my brain fumbled for the words to turn him away. Postcards. I squinted. Of Syria. All written on in English.

I looked up at him bewildered. The fog cleared and I thanked him with all my remaining enthusiasm. His pleasure, he replied and left. I must have dropped them in the street. Maybe the lobby. I still felt deathly ill, but Ankara was not far away. I lay in bed listening to a late-night bar thumping across the rooftops. Turkish dance music became my sweet, welcoming lullaby.

Final Decision

The spirit of adventure had been beaten out of me by that last travel mishap. When I returned from the Syria trip at 7:30 a.m. on Monday, I went directly to the classroom. This had been the plan all along, but I hadn't counted on the illness and the sleepless night ride. My nausea never let up for a moment and despite the stifling heat and stagnant air of the bus, the Turkish aversion to drafts prevented anyone from opening the vents along the ceiling. I stared with dismay at the many passengers who dozed calmly in sweaters. I explained my problem to two young med students sitting in front of me. "How many days did you take this medicine?" Seven. "You must take this medicine for ten days!" "Yes, yes," the other agreed. "Ten days at least. Maybe fourteen."

After an excruciating day in front of class in some sort of adrenaline hallucination, I went home to begin the medicine I should have taken before the trip. This time it was ten days and it delivered everything it promised: the cure *and* the long list of side effects. I missed Tuesday, unable to lift the covers with my fatigued limbs. Then the metal taste returned, the dizziness, the headache. Then came sharp joint pain and stiffness and I clutched the banister in the stairwell as I eased down the stairs like an old arthritic. Even holding a pen became a challenge. The very last item on the list of side effects was depression. I almost laughed wondering who *wouldn't* be depressed after such a list of miseries.

That was the final straw. I began to think seriously about returning to the States.

But in all of this I never felt alone. Chad covered my classes without complaint when it was necessary. My students, who could see my condition, went a little easier on me; my pleading with them for order was done with weary sighs and frowns. A look in a student's direction was enough to elicit an apology and a moment's pause in his or her chatter. Several days after my return, İffet, who had watched me with concern from day to day and made sure I was taking my medicine, leaned into my classroom to tell me the Mooder wanted to see me. I thought perhaps my teaching was suffering and I was about to be reprimanded.

I entered his office timidly. "You wanted to see me?"

He stood behind his desk, as imposing as ever, and looked at me seriously. "Come here." Bewildered, I stepped closer and he gestured me around the desk. He stepped up next to me and grabbed the waist of my pants and tugged me around like a rag doll. He said something to İffet.

"He says you have lost a lot of weight and wants to know if you need anything."

I smiled sheepishly at his Sultan's concern. "I'm OK now; I have been taking my medicine."

He ordered me to eat more and I was dismissed.

Later that week CNN brought more gloom to my days. From the internet lab I went to a dance demonstration in the gymnasium. I found several of my students standing in the back row, rising up on their toes for a better view. I watched their adorable faces; some of them came to kiss me on both cheeks. I watched them more than the dancers, fully absorbing their innocence. Only two days before, back in America, two children had gone to school with automatic weapons for a shooting spree. Some of the Turkish teachers asked us about it, horrified by such unconscionable violence. I felt they looked at me with uncertainty, wondering about my culture, that land of plenty where the children are terrorists without a cause. What kind of country could breed such savage children? I wondered what kind of place I'd be going back to.

I finished the dosage and took another trip to the lab to make sure I was cured. The side effects soon cleared up, but the funk into which I had descended had left its scars. If I had previously been uncertain about staying in Turkey, I now became downright desperate to be gone from the place. My spirits weakened, I became horribly impatient with the discipline problems. Any little setback - a long line at the phone company, the postal woman's impatience with my Turkish - sent me home weary and frustrated. I began to lose interest even in going out. But I had agreed to a two-year contract in Izmir. For days I walked around in a nervous titter feeling my reservations turning to panic.

I sat by the phone taking deep breaths to summon up my nerve. I understood I hadn't signed anything, but the fact was I had said yes and so had wasted two weeks of his time for finding someone else. Chad told me I was nuts, that the director was sure to understand. Linda reassured me that he surely must have someone else on his list. That's Turkey, Chad pointed out. He had a point. Obviously an experienced director was prepared for the inevitable setbacks of international teaching and the particular hassles that Turkey often provided.

I called the director and told him. He sighed and said he understood. In fact, he added that he had done the same thing after his first overseas job—packed it up and went Stateside. He stayed only a year and then left and never looked back. That was twenty-five years ago.

When I hung up the phone, I could feel the difference.

The tautness in my chest let go; it felt as though my lungs had increased in capacity. Like slipping into a hot bath, my body relaxed and my mind followed with it. Sometimes our reasons for the decisions we make don't add up on paper. I had turned down a very good paying job with excellent benefits in an exotic land to return to the land of my discontent and possibly not find a permanent position. The king would once again become pauper. Money would return to being an issue. The job search would be extremely difficult from where I was, but I knew, somehow, that I was doing the right thing. It just *felt* that way.

I still moved glumly about the apartment, but I was not alone. Chad and Bob knew when to give a guy some space. They also knew when not to. On Friday night, when I declined an invitation to a party at Cedric's, they insisted. And when I arrived, my gloom began to dissolve. Friends asked about my health and talked about my Syria pictures which were making the rounds. A little laughter and music started things the other way. Making new friends that night was a reminder that there was still a lot to discover.

By the end of the evening, I had turned a corner. Bob had introduced me to an attractive university student with a passion for literature, and the night had slipped away. In the early hours, I crawled into my bed feeling lighter and with a phone number penned across my palm.

The Black Sea

May 19th, National Youth Day and Atatürk's adopted birthday, was yet another holiday and the school gave everyone two days off. Massaging the Müdür's ego got us leave for the school day sandwiched between holiday and weekend. We told him we wanted to see the Black Sea and Giresun—his hometown. Everyone would know him there, he told us. We laughed a little and then realized he was serious.

On the overnight bus, I awoke as we passed through beautiful valleys wrapped in wisps of morning fog as the morning's gold slid like honey down green hills and ragged rocky outcroppings. Pockets of lush green sprouted up among hills and ravines. We arrived in Samsun on the coast and watched the morning unfold over the Black Sea.

A strange combination of fresh and salt water, it is believed to be a former lake turned sea around 7,000 years ago when the narrow land where Istanbul is now let loose and allowed the salty waters of the Aegean and Mediterranean to rush through. The shoreline may have expanded up to a mile or two inland in a matter of days, no doubt terrifying any human settlements and covering much of their world in a flood some believe inspired the many regional stories that predate the Noah story. What exists there today are fishing ports and a coastline green with agriculture, including tea, tobacco and cherry trees.

In Samsun we grabbed breakfast and agreed just to go as far as we could and turn back. A few places were must-sees:

199

Giresun, Trabzon, Sumela monastery, and Tirebolu, where we would look up a fellow teacher's family. Following the coast in the first available bus, we stopped at a few roadside attractions with our itinerary never being more intense than "Let's get to Giresun by the end of the day."

On a *dolmuş* continuing east we followed the highway as it twisted along between a rising slope of trees and a beachless shore. The wide blue water frothed white along broken rock. We slipped through short tunnels and passed intermittent clumps of red-roofed houses. I read a sign in Turkish: Don't be a traffic monster. I had been told before that everyone has known someone who has been lost to the traffic monster. Now I was no exception—while I was in Syria, the school nurse had died in a car accident on her holiday. Turkey loses more people in one day to traffic fatalities than it would in a small war. And in keeping with the kismet tradition, the people perceive each accident as a matter of fate rather than fault.

Turks in Ankara had warned me about the accent in the north, but oddly enough, I found it clearer than ever. It seemed slower, and the vowels more distinguishable. A corpulent man with a sizable gray moustache turned around from the front seat to face me, his arm over the back of the seat. He wanted to know what I thought of his country. As many had already, he asked me if I was Christian; I shrugged and said yes to avoid sorting it out. He was Muslim of course. But on the subject of the Koran he had this to say: "The Koran doesn't make people good. Look at Egypt!" I wondered if Turkey would ever be able to leave behind the worry of losing the reins to a religious government.

Turkey is sometimes frowned upon for coups that have occurred in its past, when the military stepped in and pushed out elected governments. The religious powers of Turkey have at times won the elections. The world has seen what happened to Iran and Afghanistan when fundamentalist regimes took over. Turkey, for its part, was founded on a secular government. Atatürk even went so far as to abolish the fez and veil in his time. There are many who fear that a religious administration would overturn the constitution, and that all democratic gains would be lost. It frightens me when Americans get careless about keeping religion and government separate in our own country; it is a slippery slope. At Büyük Kolej, a private school in a 99% Muslim country, there is no organized prayer. Why not? Who are they protecting? Neighbors like Iran and Saudi Arabia provide the answer to that.

The *dolmuş* dropped us off at the small harbor of Giresun, full of small fishing vessels and two lumbering freighters. We found ourselves a musty but spacious room above a brick alleyway and then Bob and I headed down to the waterfront. The sun was quickly slipping behind the opposite curve of the small bay and we ventured out onto the breakwater to watch the finale. On either side of the wall were massive concrete blocks the size of minivans that seemed to have been cast aside as a Titan's playthings. Groups of older men sat on several of the level ones, drinking *rakı* and having a small picnic. They had taken off their shoes and were laughing loudly to the wind. The breakwater pointed west and to our left the fishing boats were tied up for the night. Beyond them the city, tightly packed, rose up the hillside in a chaotic arrangement that somehow created order. High above, to the east, ensconced in vines and trees, the remains of a medieval castle sat upon a promontory that divided the city.

The sun drooped over small mountains which rose among wisps of fog. Fisherman slipped along the darkening waters, their silhouettes casting long shadows. The waves surged in and out like the uneven breaths of a fever dream—powerful,

yet not strong enough to break high over the blocks of concrete. The sun sank into a haze that swallowed much of its
color and all of its shape.

For dinner, we found a seafood restaurant not far from our
room. Mehmet Garipoğlu, the owner, moved his finger along
the glass of the refrigerated display and we cried out at every
stop: What's this? And this? This? He patiently tried to
explain. Finally, he just smiled, revealing wide gaps in the
sides of his teeth, and in a deep voice told us not to worry.
Going on the sixth-sense vibe, we resigned ourselves to his
good judgement. And his judgement was *very* good. The first
things to the table were the bottle of *rakı* and a platter of
roasted hazelnuts. We asked him if he knew the Mooder. He
frowned and we repeated the name a few times, but he just
shrugged.

In spite of our failure with name dropping, he joined us for
most of the meal. This one rated as one of the best. Good
company, and fish cooked in butter with diced onions and
tomatoes that melted in my mouth. We raved and Mehmet
basked in our praise. As we sipped some Turkish coffee we
explained where we lived. He would be in Ankara in the summer and asked if he could look us up. We insisted. If we were
still in Ankara, our house was his house.

In the morning Mehmet fed us another buttery meal and
refused to charge us, and then we were off to the castle. Not
much is left of its old fortifications, and of those still standing,
vines and moss have blended them into the trees and grasses
that are the last remaining besiegers.

The walls fascinated me. I always imagine how I might
penetrate the defenses if I were an invading army, or how I
might maintain them if I were under siege. No doubt for
those who built them this was the primary concern. Anyone
who claimed theirs unbreachable would have been highly
optimistic. In the same way, we protect our lifestyles, either

the grandiose ideals of freedom or fiefdom, or the very basic ones of family and loyalties. It is a foolish notion that we can pile stones and mortar around ourselves so that we might keep out change, stop the advancing armies of life that always want to push us back or forward, or at least out of our entrenched routines. At the very least, we are forced to keep replacing loose stones, filling in the cracks in our resolve. But just as it has been for that castle, change is inexorable.

Giresun was, along with Izmir, one of the last footholds Greek soldiers held before being repelled during the struggle for Turkish independence. A small monument stands as a reminder. Down the hill we found an old church-turned-museum, and after a cursory review of armor, weaponry, and pottery, we stepped out into a downpour. We ran along the road back toward our hotel beneath flashes of lightning. We ducked into a restaurant and ate soup, waiting to dry off a bit before gathering our things from the hotel and seeking out the next *dolmuş* up the coast.

After about an hour of intermittently slumping against Bob and jerking awake, I looked up to see the sign for Tirebolu, a town of only about 15,000. The coastal highway passed beneath a steep slope of housing and we stepped off in the middle of town, where a small renovated fort thrust out into the sea. Arzu Yanıkömer, a fellow teacher, had grown up in Tirebolu, and, in fact, her family still lived there. She had given us a short list of ideas for pensions, restaurants, and tourist sites. We found Eren Pansiyon from the list and deposited our bags.

Our Turkish had become comfortable and our inaccuracy in pronunciation, I think, ironically prevented us from being baffled by the accent of the region. I noticed some usage differences as well. In Giresun, a Turkish woman had used "*ne*" as "no" rather than "what." Arzu had advised us to speak as much Turkish as possible. Good advice for any place in

Turkey. People became very friendly, or rather, much friendlier.

The pension owner knew the Yanıkömer family. Bob used
the phone to try to reach Arzu's brother, but no one
answered, so we walked to the tea garden just outside the fort.
The waiter picked up a small table and three stools and we followed him out onto the rocks along the water's edge. We
toasted another sunset with tea.

The buildings of the town were packed tightly together as
usual and the rooftops were staggered up the verdant hills. It
never seemed like these towns were sprawling. There was
something quaint even about Ankara in that it huddled
together, seemingly slowing its encroachment on the open
spaces around it. The Turks' ability to build *anywhere*
astounds me still.

The twilight was fading and we rose to pay our bill. As we
were leaving, we asked the young man managing the place if
he knew Ahmet, Arzu's brother. "Of course! He is my friend.
He is coming right now." So we waited. He ordered *pide* for
us on the phone and when it arrived we ate it out on the rocks
on the pages of a newspaper spread over the table.

A tall young man showed up and the manager pointed him
to us. The eyes, the smile, the long nose with the bend in it—
no question: this was Arzu's brother. He greeted us as though
we were long-lost cousins whose arrival had been talked about
for months. He spoke no English but with Bob's lead especially, we were able to converse.

We chatted a long while about what was in town and
where he worked, and about things we might see the next
day. When we rose to leave, he sneaked off and paid the *pide*
bill, refusing our money when we discovered what he'd done.
As we made our way up the hillside streets, we passed several
people who stopped to exchange pleasantries with Ahmet and
to satisfy their small-town curiosities about the three

strangers. I loved knowing my butcher, my grocer, the neighborhood cop. I could spend so much time fleeing a small town in Wisconsin only to find myself yearning to duplicate it.

The old houses were made of wood rather than of the more common concrete. Some of them had no floors inside at all and some were being torn down for new buildings. Ahmet showed us a few up close, turning to us for our commiseration—ornate wooden trim and gables, fresh coats of paint. "You see? Curtains in the windows. No floors, but curtains." The town kept a nice facade on these places until they were destroyed. But was it an obsession with appearances or simply small-town pride, I wondered. "Do you want to see *my* home?" he asked. The answer in Ahmet's case was pride.

After spending so much time in Ankara, I had forgotten what it meant to have a *house*. Ahmet's house bespoke his disdain for the trampling of old wooden buildings. We climbed hillside steps up to a slender three-story affair. The gray siding would have given it a sort of sinister look had it not been for the colorful flower garden skirting the foundation and a modest copse along the yard's edge. I turned around and could see all the way down the slope to where the fort thrust out into the water, bathed in soft yellow floodlights.

Arzu's parents greeted us at the door with embraces. We took off our shoes and climbed a staircase that creaked gently under our steps. Each board had been rounded and shaped by so many feet before ours. We sat down in a parlor and tea was served. Arzu's mother and father were in their early sixties and bubbled over with the same friendliness for which Arzu could be counted on. Another younger brother, Mehmet, emerged and sat on the arm of the sofa. I looked from face to smiling face and in the center of every one except the mother's was that same long curving nose and its bump in the center. I set my tea on the low table before me and surveyed the room. Some black and white pictures caught my attention and Mr.

Yanıkömer told us they were his parents and his wife's parents. They could have been pictures of the couple before me dressed up in yesteryear's fashions and the mother in a veil. Arzu's mother didn't wear one.

Mr. Yanıkömer kept veering off each subject to interject commentary on the evolution of the house. It had been in his family for a long time and each generation modified it in some fashion. Back in 1915, a Russian shell had pierced the wall just below the window. "Hey, this is the first time I've been in a house hit by a cannonball," I commented in English. Mr. Yanıkömer, standing by the window, reached down and patted the plaster and smiled.

I awoke the next morning tired and with sore fingers. Some time around 11 the night before the Yanıkömers had brought out a bowl full of hazelnuts. Not having seen them unshelled before, my first thought was acorns. The father and then Mehmet showed us how to shell them without a nutcracker, by placing two into a curved finger and squeezing. We stayed on until midnight, bruising our fingers and conversing lightly. And when we finally rose to leave, they seemed terribly disappointed. They didn't let us out the door without a couple of bags of raisins and nuts for the next day's journey, as if we were family leaving home.

The next day we arrived in Trabzon, a port city originally founded in the 8th century BC. During the Crusades, when the Crusaders actually sacked fellow Christians in Constantinople, Trabzon was taken by the Byzantines Alexius and David Comnenus after they fled their fallen capital. It is home to the 13th-century church Ayasofya, which contains an assortment of fine Byzantine art. Mehmet the Conqueror took the city for the Ottomans in 1461 soon after his conquest of Constantinople. And here we were invading several centuries later, carrying off souvenirs and treasures preserved on rolls of film.

We explored the Russian market, a long pavilion of vendors peddling imports from over the nearby border of Georgia. We stared in awe at the colorful interior of Ayasofya, and lingered for a moment among its flowers outside. And for the better part of a day we went south into a verdant range of mountains to find the 12th-century Sumela monastery.

Built into the sheer face of a towering cliff, the monastery takes a bit of precarious climbing and hardy trail hiking to reach. A river runs below it and the chatter of its water is soothing like the birds and breeze through the trees. The sun poked through intermittently and we passed through a landscape as beautiful as any in Turkey.

The monastery itself felt cramped. In the main chapel the ceiling was a collection of frescoes riddled with gouges where Muslim invaders had attempted to obliterate all the faces, possibly with thrown stones. Looking out over the river valley below I thought back to Hattuşaş and its own defensive isolation. Here the isolation provided protection not only from invading armies, but also from distractions of the material world. As I went rushing around Turkey like a child in a toy store, I had trouble imagining such monotonous solitude. I was in love with the richness of the world and wanted to throw myself into it at every opportunity.

Back in Trabzon that night, we filled ourselves with wonderful seafood and went dizzy with *rakı*. Along the seashore we found a carnival and spent the rest of the evening whirling along on rides and laughing into the wind. The only thing that differed from the carnivals back home was the bumper cars. Contrary to the recklessness of the typical Turkish driver, everyone on the ride *avoided* any contact with other bumper cars. It was the damnedest thing; a dozen bumper cars frantically running from each other. I hoped for the same for the long bus trip home the next morning.

Cappadocia with a Friend

We arrived at night, so the landscape only revealed itself in the small glowing pockets of intermittent streetlights and the graceful sweeps of the headlights as we rode the weaving highway to the town of Göreme. Behind the faintly reflected image of a gaping, wide-eyed American teacher, another world, full of giant, rocky teeth, slipped past. I most certainly left my face imprinted on the window glass as I struggled to perceive the landscape. When the bus came around the sloping bend of the road into town, the lights there revealed a most curious sight.

Fairy chimneys, they are often called. Spires of soft stone naturally made by wind and rain over the years. A landscape like a mouthful of rotten teeth. Mars. The moon. Certainly not Turkey. Interspersed amongst small houses and stores were conical outcroppings, ranging from the size of a small truck to about three stories high. The uniformity of the shapes is what struck me first, but then the details began to emerge. Doorways. Windows. Stairs. Power lines. These were not simply part of the landscape, they were homes, some abandoned and some still pouring out a warm but eerie light. Our bus stopped briefly and Ayşe and I were the only two to get off in what was downtown Göreme. Except for a couple of restaurants, all the businesses were closed.

I had met Ayşe at Cedric's party weeks before. A staunch atheist, she was the only child of two medical professionals, former participants in the leftist movements of the '70s. Her mother had seen fellow communists have their eyes put out; her father had been blackballed at the university for a time. So unlike many around her, she was not rebelling against a religious upbringing; on the contrary, she had been raised to disdain it. And her firm feminist beliefs were a reminder to me that I had met many women of her generation and the generation before who were going to guarantee that Turkey didn't leave its female population behind.

High walls, closely built homes, and the curving and steep road from the square prevented us from seeing where we were heading. Only a small sign at the bottom of a walled staircase told us that we had arrived: Kelebek Pansiyon. Butterfly Pension.

We ascended to a patio and my excitement manifested itself in a chuckle. "What IS this place?" Three patios of varying levels rested between four towering fairy chimneys. Steps went this way and that and an office and small restaurant sat above it all and to the right. A woman alone in the kitchen told us to go down to the bar, which was apparently just off the first patio. We descended again and I opened a wooden door into what for all appearances was a well-lit cave with a full bar. A blond woman in her fifties looked up from behind the bar and smiled. She spoke English with a British accent and initially it made me feel as though some of the authenticity had been rubbed off. But when she showed us our room, all was forgotten. I stepped down into another cave with two beds in it.

"This is all we have, but there is a double bed opening up tomorrow." She left us and I flopped down onto a bed, fascinated. There was an extra third bed in an alcove in the wall and everything else rested on a hollow hardwood floor made to fit the odd shape of the stone and strewn with rugs.

With a bottle of a local sweet wine, we sat on the rooftop

patio, joked about being on Jupiter and debated whether one could see Earth from where we were sitting. As I peered at the horizon, I could just make out the teeth of a giant's saw outlined in stars.

The following morning, the view of Jupiter had brightened into a range of stony colors not quite as brilliant as the Grand Canyon, but no less stunning in their arrangement. Throughout the town, situated down the hill from the hotel, conical stone formations thrust up among businesses and houses. The fairy chimneys were no less exotic in daylight, but now I could see more variety in their shape. Almost as common as the giant stalagmite was a formation that, no matter how innocent or naive, one could only call a giant phallus.

Ayşe finished her tea, I grabbed my camera bag, and we headed for the stairs. The valley was just about a mile outside of town and we decided to walk. In the fourth century Christians found the desolation and seclusion of Cappadocia fitting for monastic life, and many moved there and built churches that from the outside looked like cliff faces and rocky outcroppings.

We ventured from the roadway and followed a dusty path up into low-lying hills in search of the appropriately named Hidden Church. As we came up over a rise, we found a boy and his donkey. I shouted *merhaba* and he waved. When we finally came to the peak of the ridge, we found—nothing. We paced along the crest, glancing down the drop-off on the other side, searching for clues. Moments later the boy joined us. He was Süleyman. A good name, I told him. He told us he could show us the church.

He went to the edge and dropped down a few feet to a narrow foothold and beckoned us to follow. Beyond where he stood was a slight turn back into the slope and room for one person to sneak by and down to a narrow ledge. When I landed, he showed me our prize: a narrow cave opening with steel bars across it. Inside was nothing even as explicit as our hotel room.

Back at the road I withdrew a few lira bills and offered them to the boy. He stared at them confusedly and then his eyes flew wide and he shook his head. "But you were our guide," I explained. "I pay you for your work." After what was more resistance than simple courtesy demanded, he accepted my offer. We passed through an open stretch of meager farmland across which lay the opening to the valley. Two women and an older man worked a potato field with hand tools. Süleyman set his animal loose and whistled to the people who all stood up from their work and waved. He left the road, beckoning us to follow. His father, mother, and older sister greeted us enthusiastically. The boy's sister's name was Ayşe too. We stood smiling at each other and I wondered at the contrast: Ayşe worked in the dirt before us, her hair loosely veiled, while my friend stood in shorts and a tank top. In some ways this was the breadth of the cultural divide. But I felt no irony in their smiles, no discomfort in their affability.

Ahmet, Süleyman's father, plucked some small fruit called *erik* from a nearby tree. I took a bite from what resembled a hard, green apple in texture and color, and a small plum in shape and size. The flesh was sour and not very juicy but I ate it politely. We sat on a path of packed-down dirt and chatted about simple things like the weather, the tourists, and my home, Ankara.

After our snack, we resumed our hike into the valley with Süleyman continuing as a guide. The valley opened up like the land of a fairy tale. I could imagine dwarves and hobbits, dragons and fairies passing among the trails and staircases that only emerged from their surroundings when we were practically on top of them. As the sun rose, the stone became painfully white. The road passed through the park itself and in the center was a small visitor's pavilion.

The first site I ducked into was a church. The ceiling rose up twenty feet and the walls were painted in simple frescoes. All the eyes or faces of the figures had been gouged out by Muslim invaders long ago. In the center was an altar, fashioned from the stone of the hill into which it was carved. I looked down into a steep metal staircase that led to a sub-cavern, also with richly colored walls.

In the sub-cavern were kneelers. No fooling, I thought, these were really churches. Returning to the path outside, we continued exploring, passing in and out of long-abandoned dwellings, a few small series of caves and tunnels. Without the extras that we had back at the hotel, they looked cold and foreboding. Süleyman kept pace with us, and often climbed ahead to determine whether we needed to bother with the effort to see them.

Outside of a special site, Ayşe refused to pay an entry fee. Her explanation was that the conservative religious political parties in the area would use that to fund their party. I argued that certainly *some* of the money must have been put back into restoration. As we debated, I handed my money to the guard, and without my awareness—and to Ayşe's chagrin—he took the price of both tickets. I bit my lip, but she scowled with a forced sigh and we entered anyway.

I wouldn't argue with her regarding possible misappropriation of funds, but it was undeniable that the place had received a significant makeover. It was called the Dark Church, because it was sunk deep into the stone and far from any external light source. But despite want of the sun this place glowed in the most vivid colors I had seen yet. The caverns were low over our heads and too small to hold more than a dozen people. But every inch of the curving walls told a story. I took Ayşe around the room, pointing out various stories from the Gospels, the Crucifixion and Judas' betrayal, and interpreting some of the symbols among the drawings. The

213

bright human figures were balanced out by a rich blue background full of rivers and hills and geometric designs.

Süleyman caught up with us outside. The hot sun sent Süleyman and me to wash our faces and arms in a fountain. As we sat on the curb drying ourselves, he made the decision to rename me. My Turkish name would be Mehmet.

I pointed to myself like Tarzan: "Mehmet?"

"*Evet,*" he nodded eagerly.

As we passed the visitor center, I noticed a freezer full of ice cream treats. Süleyman resisted my offer for ice cream but this time you could see it was killing him. He finally broke down, almost with relief, and pointed to his selection down in the icy depths.

We returned to Süleyman's family and Ahmet insisted we take a small stone carving the size of a fist that resembled a clump of mushrooms stretched lengthwise. He had made it himself and he never broke down and accepted our offer of payment. He insisted: it was a gift. I took a picture of the entire family before we departed, waving, with Ahmet's address in my pocket.

"The next place, Zelve, is ten kilometers. We can hitchhike."

I felt awkward with my thumb in the air, still effectively conditioned by my mother that only psychopaths—axe murderers and the like—hitchhike or pick up hitchhikers. Fifteen minutes later, a Mercedes slowed down for us, and we stepped up to the window announcing our destination. The two men driving were very friendly and we hopped into the back seat. Our highway hosts were heading past the turnoff to Zelve, but insisted on taking us the extra kilometer or so off their course to drop us off directly. Once again our lira donation was refused.

We entered another valley that split into two distinct branches. Within each were deep ravines and an assortment of cave-homes. Dusty paths wove through tall dry grass that rustled gently in the breeze. We spent a couple hours photographing each other and the land. Wild flowers of bright red and electric blue made vivid contrast with the warm but sandy-colored stone. As we ascended the trail we could see out the end of the valley where rich farmland spread out toward the horizon, occasionally broken by rock formations. I sat in the sun, staring across the ravine, attempting to discern the hidden dwellings in the cliff face. From time to time voices carried on the wind as though from the belly of a beast and moments later a head would emerge like a pigeon from its dwelling high up along a ridge that at first glance hadn't looked traversable. Ayşe held up the back of her hand to show me something. I moved closer to observe a ladybug sunning itself on her knuckle.

"They bring good luck here. Do they bring good luck in the United States too?"

"Well, we consider them special, yes."

I watched her as she watched the tiny creature flex its secret wings and slide away through the tall grass.

On our way out to the highway we bought another small bottle of the sweet wine and had the shopkeeper loosen the cork. I packed it away in my camera bag. We hitched the short ride back toward town, stopping at a village called Çavuşin. With a couple more local children as guides we climbed into another old rock dwelling which had once been the Church of St. John the Baptist. As recently as the 1960s people had lived in these caves. But the erosion that created the hills didn't see any reason to stop just because people moved in. By the end of the '60s, several people had been killed by collapsing abodes and the government had forced many to move their families for safety's sake.

Rose Valley was the last site of the day and one of the boys took us along a back road through olive orchards and past a cemetery. The graves were on a small rise along the road, and already the sun was dipping behind the headstones. The road seemed clear as it crossed into young vineyards of loose, well-tilled soil, so we sent our guide on his way with a generous tip. The sun sinking behind us caused the stone to fill with warmer tones. Unlike the tall spires or the jagged valleys, these were lower to the earth and softly rounded as though made of marshmallow. Our feet sank into the loose soil as we threaded our way through trees and patches of vineyard to the base of the stone.

Ayşe insisted we go on, while I felt it looked like a dead end. We agreed to continue to the next bend down a road of tire ruts. We met a man walking out to his car. He offered us a ride into Göreme if we would be around in fifteen minutes. He also recommended yet another church. We found it tucked up into the low ridge and we decided to give the church idea just one more chance.

The caves were quite open to the outside, which allowed us enough light to see a few badly worn and faded frescoes. I opened the wine and Ayşe was fascinated by the thought of drinking alcohol in a holy place, something unheard of in a mosque. When I told her it was actually part of the mass she found it amusing. I kissed her and she jokingly pushed me away, casting her eyes about in the growing darkness as though we would be discovered. "I suppose you can do that in a church as well?"

"Weddings. Sometimes my parents used to kiss at the sign of peace."

"You naughty Christians. What's the sign of peace?"

"Well... towards the end of mass you greet the guy sitting next you and say 'Peace' or 'Peace be with you.'" We looked at each other and started laughing. "Geez, what was so normal before seems strange when I hear it out of my own mouth."

The frescoes faded into the shadows and we set out for the long walk back to Göreme. As promised, the management had switched our room to a double. Unlike the previous cave that seemed buried under the hotel, this room was itself a cone of rock. The carved stairs climbed up between two fairy chimneys and we stepped into one of them. Exhausted, we collapsed on the bed. Across the ceiling against a white background was a large red cross. Our room had once been a chapel. Ayşe directed her thoughts toward the ceiling: "Is there anything that you're *not* supposed to do in a church?"

Graduation and the
Magic Window Closes

The eighth-graders clutched their mortarboards to their heads as they scrambled in and out of the locker room, which doubled as a sort of dressing room before the ceremony. They wore satin blue robes and striped scarves bearing the other two school colors of red and white. Each teacher would take turns handing out diplomas and the four students I was matched with ran up to me with big smiles. In the gymnasium the stands were already filling up. The lights were low except for over the five groups of empty chairs across the gym floor, each group corresponding to the five separate classes of eighth-graders.

The final couple of weeks had passed like a dream. Grades were handed in early, so the final classes were assumed to be lost. We watched movies in English and talked about them. Students asked me about plans, exchanged e-mails with me, and occasionally begged me to reconsider. 8E—the class I had thought I'd dread—composed a scrapbook filled with photos and magazine clippings and cartoons that either warned me I wasn't allowed to leave or reminded me that I would never be forgotten. It came as a surprise when I realized how much I was going to miss them.

I had set aside several nights to go around Ankara and say farewell to all my friends. I bid farewell to Hale at a different club; Temptation bar had switched ownership. Birsen, Canan,

Cedric, Shala—it was strange to leave their apartments know-ing I might never see them again. Chad, Bob and I had taken photos with the men at the local market, with the Mooder, some of the fellow teachers, the two Ebrus, Dilek, and a few notably friendly janitors in their Oompa Loompa uniforms. On the way home from school, I stopped to say goodbye to Hasan the Police Officer. He had brought me one of his Grateful Dead-looking police patches as something to remember him by.

By the night of graduation, Bob was already off traveling with his parents and Chad and I were performing our final duty. The lights dimmed to nearly nil and a spotlight drew all eyes to the stage at the end of the gymnasium. Music began. Not "Pomp and Circumstance" but the thumping beat of a dance song. Fog poured onto the stage and it became a glow-ing mass of white. A red carpet lined with tiny lights like the aisles in movie theaters led from the cloud to the chairs on the gym floor. The first graduate burst from the fog proudly as the music became louder. This event had nothing in common with the often painfully boring decorum of commencement in the U.S., which usually seems more a funeral than a celebra-tion. Six students shared the top honors and they were called one by one to stand in front of the seated classes. When each honored student took his or her stand, there was a soft pop overhead; a hail of confetti and balloons drifted down as a banner unrolled with each name written vertically in shining letters. Dilek leaned over to me and asked me if graduation was anything like this in the United States. I couldn't even draw my eyes from it all, but only shook my head no. Speeches were given by three of the honored students: one in Turkish, one in English, and one in German.

Then the long handing out of diplomas. I watched with interest as each Turkish teacher rose to his or her duty. The amount of applause seemed a good indication of that teacher's popularity. Those who evoked standing ovations were no surprise, as I had heard the students referring to them frequently, and in the faculty lounge one could tell who was most down-to-earth and loved his job. What did come as a surprise was the roar that met my ears when I stepped up to the walkway. The entire eighth-grade class rose to its feet. I distributed the diplomas to the four students and then kissed each one on both cheeks before turning to face the school photographer. I sat down with my heart beating madly. Chad received the same ovation.

Afterward, the crowd burst into the lower garden outside, where the cafeteria staff stood behind a couple long tables of punch and pastries. Everyone turned their eyes to the sky to watch some light fireworks. The street in front of the school flashed green, red, and yellow, and the tiny explosions echoed off the storefronts. Some residents had come out onto their apartment balconies to watch the spectacle. I wandered around, taking pictures of my students. Some laughed, some cried, and we all embraced. Some pleaded with me with furrowed brows, "Teacher, please don't gooooo!"

An hour after the ceremony, the crowd had thinned out some. İffet and her mother and sister sat along the wall of the garden, and Chad and I asked them to pose for a picture. I hugged İffet tightly, "Well, Mom, thank you for everything. You were great." I was tired and felt nostalgic before I had even left the building. It was time to head home and finish packing. "I'll see you guys...." I froze, halfway turned to the gate. I frowned, as did Chad. "Hey, wait a minute." We both realized that was the last time we'd see each other in Turkey. Chad was leaving for the weekend and I would be flying out before his return. We hugged each other tightly for a moment, half-amazed the year was actually ending.

"One more drink," he suggested.

We walked to a liquor store and splurged on a bottle of

Bailey's Irish Cream. When we arrived back at the school, we stopped at what was already the *former* Lights Market where a veiled woman gave us a couple of plastic cups and smiled, waving us away when we offered our money. Erdal had disappeared somehow without our noticing. Right next door was the empty lot Chad and I had discovered at the beginning of the school year, the opening that afforded the framed view of Ankara at night and the mountains beyond during the day. The place where I had periodically stopped to meditate after a long day of classes. Someone had begun a new apartment building. Spaces needed to be filled. The oak tree was gone. Even the slope had been dug up and a foundation of concrete lurked there in the dark with the spindly whiskers of reinforcing steel cables protruding from it.

It was as quiet as ever, but the atmosphere was different. Whereas before it held a peaceful inactivity, now it spoke of inexorable change. The rising structure would soon block the view, and the street would become just another anonymous path through Ankara. The low wall along the walk had already been torn up and replaced by a temporary shelter for the workers' tools. Chad and I sat on a couple of concrete blocks and poured out our last drinks in plastic.

I still have photographs of our Magic Window. They are lost among all the other more exotic shots in my photo album. Friends pass over them for the magnificence of a mosque or the glitter of the sea. But that empty lot encapsulates something much more personal: the bittersweet reminder of life's ephemeral pleasures, of opportunities that pass. And as I sat there that night, sighing at the constructed clutter in my view, I felt a sense of closure. These experiences would never be repeated and for that I was sad to see them go. But I also relished in the pricelessness of things so unique. That which can be duplicated loses its gold.

We are the creators of our lives. We form them from whatever material presents itself. Just as the banality of the photos compelled the looker to turn the page, I was made to consider that it truly could have been any street. And I promised myself to search out another and make it too my own.